# The Layman's Guide to Smoking Cessation

## Anthony Parkinson, D.C.

The Layman's Guide to Smoking Cessation

Address:
140 Sagefield Square
Canton, MS 39046

For more information on this book, please visit the website: http//www.lulu.com/AnthonyParkinson

ISBN: 978-1-4357-0214-1

# Table of Contents

# INTRODUCTION

When you first started smoking, it seemed like a cool, hip, sexy way of expressing your personality. All the coolest people you knew smoked, such as rock stars, movie stars, artists, thinkers, etc. etc. So why not you?

But now you're not so sure. It doesn't seem so cool to smoke anymore. Everyone around you has quit, and it seems like you're some kind of outcast. You want to change. You want to break the habit – butt out, and stay out.

But every time you've tried to quit, something happens (and you don't really know what) and you end up smoking again. You want to break the cycle, but don't really know how.

If you've had a hard time trying to quit (and staying smoke free), then this book is for you. This book will give you an actual program that you can follow to understand your own personal reasons to quit. And this book will help you cope with the habit and addiction of smoking, and it will make sure you stay off cigarettes for good.

Of course, you're probably wondering why this book should work for you, when there are so many quit-smoking programs and guides out there.

The reason why this book will work for you is that it recognizes your individuality. In order to quit smoking, you need to know why you smoke in the first place, and then you need to know what people, places or things trigger your unique urge to light up.

You may have many personal reasons to smoke:

• You may be under a lot of stress at work.
• All of your friends smoke, so you can't escape.
• Smoking helps you keep your weight down.
• You are strongly addicted to cigarettes.
• You enjoy smoking and it is really a pleasurable activity for you.
• You don't have the willpower to quit.
• Smoking helps you feel relaxed and positive.

Once you know why you smoke, you can start working toward overcoming your individual obstacles – this is the surest road to become a nonsmoker for life. But you know that quitting is not actually the hardest part – the hardest part is sticking to it. The first two weeks are the hardest, and after that the first two months. This book will show you how to cope.

Congratulations! You're about to become a nonsmoker. This book is your first step toward quitting. You are on your way to doing one of the best things you can do for yourself, and the people around you. Welcome to the smoke free life.

# THE PROFILE OF A SMOKER – THIS IS YOU

As you might suspect; smokers come in all varieties and attitudes. But generally speaking, there's a lot of confusion and conflict about the role that smoking plays in the lives of smokers.

On the one hand, they see smoking as a pleasant, relaxing and helpful personal ritual that provides unidentifiable benefits. On the other hand, smokers know that smoking is a serious health-hazard, which in all likelihood will end up killing them.

Let's look at some of the typical varieties of smokers and see if you are one of these.

## 1. The Health-Concerned Smoker:

This type of smoker is very much aware of the dangers of smoking and all the many negative side effects. However, he/she still cannot bring himself to quit. Experts believe that if you quit today, you will easily add seven years to your life.

## 2. Smokers Who Feel Guilty:

Many smokers feel guilty about their habit. And these feelings increase the longer they smoke. Those who tried to quit and failed feel guilty far more than those who have not tried to quit. And smokers who have children at home feel the guiltiest because they are "polluting" the air their children breathe. Guilt can often turn into self-hatred.

## 3. Smokers Who Respect Nonsmokers:

Many smokers are very sensitive to other people who do not smoke. A large majority of smokers refrain from smoking when they are with people who do not smoke, and most ask for permission to smoke while visiting a nonsmoking friend.

In fact, many smokers feel that smoking should be regulated or banned at the workplace.

## 4. Smoking As A Working Class Habit:

Among the general population, it is now understood that the more affluent and better educated people do not smoke. It is estimated that 50% of men who have blue-collar jobs smoke, compared to 26% of professional men. Also, some 32% of those who did not graduate from high school smoked, while the figure for college graduates was only 19%. In other words, smoking is a blue collar habit, since fewer people in white collar professions smoke.

## 5. Smokers As A Persecuted Minority:

Since there is a widespread change in attitude toward smoking, many smokers feel like a persecuted minority. Many smokers point to smoking as creating a problem in their romantic relationships, even leading to breakup.

## 6. Antismoker Discrimination In The Workplace:

Many smokers feel that they are discriminated against at work because of their habit. Here is a reason behind this attitude, since smokers as a rule have a higher rate of absenteeism, they have an increased risk of death, they have decreased productivity, they have an increased rate of maintenance, and smokers damage the environment for their nonsmoking co-workers.

## 7. Smokers Want More Control:

The majority of smokers want more control over their habit. Over 90% want to quit, and about 84% have made a serious attempt at quitting.

## 8. Smokers As Outcasts:

Being a smoker nowadays is like being an outcast, because the attitudes of nonsmokers have changed drastically. Backing these attitudes is the great amount of evidence that cigarette smoke is harmful to nonsmokers.

## 9. Nonsmokers Have Become More Assertive:

In addition to their own feelings of confusion and guilt, smokers also have to deal with an increasing number of anti-smoking messages and a much more open display of anti-smoking feelings. Within recent years 39 states have passed laws prohibiting or limiting smoking in public places. Also, the National Association of Insurance Commissioners recently adopted a resolution urging insurance companies to raise smokers' insurance premiums by roughly 50%.

## 10. Why Smokers Can't Quit:

The period of withdrawal poses a powerful barrier to quitting. As well, smokers often have many positive benefits that they associate with smoking.

Here are some positive benefits that most smokers associate with smoking. Are any of these yours as well?

1) Smoking helps me deal with stressful situations.

2) Smoking gives me a pleasant and enjoyable break from work.

3) Smoking helps me unwind and relax.

4) Smoking helps me deal with painful or unpleasant situations.

5) Smoking prevents unpleasant withdrawal symptoms.

6) Smoking helps me deal with an over stimulating environment.

7) I enjoy the physical sensation of lighting and handling a cigarette.

8) Smoking increases my enjoyment of pleasant experiences.

9) Smoking helps me feel comfortable in social situations.

10) Smoking helps me concentrate.

11) Planning to Quit.

The majority of smokers believe that they will eventually quit, but they must choose their own time to quit, and most do so at a time when life is less stressful, and support for quitting is available.

12. How to Help a Smoker:

Most friends of smokers do not do a good job of helping take control of the habit. The most common strategy is to nag a smoker into quitting. But this tactic usually has the opposite effect. Nagging just makes smokers smoke more, it seems.

Here are some hints that friends can use to encourage smokers to quit:

1) Don't nag, insult, or try to shame the smoker into quitting.

2) Let the smoker know that he/she is valued as a person.

3) Listen non-judgmentally. Try to understand what benefits the smoker derives from this very seductive habit. Try to see the problem through the smokers' eyes.

4) Praise the smoker for even the smallest efforts to cut down or quit.

Perhaps you have found something that you can relate to in the twelve categories. The main point is to provide you with enough information to help you quit.

The most frequently mentioned areas of concern that smokers mention when they try to deal with quitting are the following:

1) How to stay a nonsmoker after I quit.

2) The most effective way to quit.

3) The most effective way to cut down.

4) How to get ready to quit.

5) Are there special needs for vitamins for smokers?

6) How to find out if I am a high-risk or low-risk smoker.

7) What smoking does to a smoker's body?

8) Dealing with weight gain after I quit.

9) What withdrawal symptoms will I face after I quit.

10) How can I cut my smoking risk through better stress management?

Whether you smoke or not is your choice. But to make that choice effectively you must consider your alternatives, and the benefits and hazards of each.

In quitting smoking (as in life) there are no magical cures or quick fixes. There are, however, some pretty powerful tools, many of them not widely known.

As a health-concerned smoker, you can take control of your smoking. Your spouse, family, your friends, your health care providers, and others in your home and community can provide important tools, caring, and support. But the key to success is for you to take primary responsibility to make the changes you desire.

Give yourself as much time as you need. Don't let anyone push you into attempting to quit before you feel ready.

You're going to do it your way. So let's start!

## WHY DO YOU SMOKE?

Nicotine is the only known psychoactive ingredient in tobacco smoke. Addicted smokers smoke for one principal reason – to get their accustomed doses of nicotine. Therefore, most smokers realize that smoking is addictive.

This means that when you stop smoking, you are likely to experience unpleasant symptoms such as irritability, sensitivity to sounds, light, and touch, and sudden, irrational mood changes.

Many nonsmokers think that smokers smoke only to avoid such withdrawal symptoms. But research has shown that in addition to preventing withdrawal, nicotine seems to provide a surprising variety of desirable psychological effects.

### The Rewards of Smoking

The average smoker takes ten puffs per cigarette. For the pack-a-day smoker, this works out to about 200 puffs per day. Each "hit" of nicotine reaches the smoker's brain within seven seconds, about twice as fast as a syringe full of heroin injected into a vein. Once nicotine enters the brain, it starts to mimic the brain's most powerful chemical messengers.

The result is a temporary improvement in brain chemistry that is experienced by the smoker as enhanced pleasure, decreased anxiety, and a state of alert relaxation.

As a result of this positive reinforcement many dozens of times per day, smoking becomes thoroughly a part of every aspect of the smoker's life.

These positive effects of smoking explain why the smoking habit holds its victims in such a tenacious grip.

Most smokers will say that smoking helps them concentrate, keeps them from being bored, and helps reduce the perceived level of tension in their lives. As well, smoking helps them cope with an over-stimulating environment, gives them positive pleasure, helps them relax, reduces their feeling of distress, helplessness, and loneliness, helps them keep weight down, and makes them feel more at ease in social situations.

Smoking can even provide a burst of energy when feeling tired, and can even help a smoker concentrate more effectively. In fact, smoking helps a smoker control his moods.

These "rewards" of smoking go a long way toward minimizing the negative consequences, and an even longer way toward ensuring that the act of smoking will be repeated again and again, until it becomes a habit so well ingrained that you do it without even thinking about it. But smoking is not just a habit – it is also an addiction.

The nicotine in cigarettes is a powerful addictive drug that makes smokers feel good. Each time you smoke, the positive biological effects of nicotine add to all the other positive rewards of smoking, which makes the smoking habit even stronger.

The Effects of Nicotine

Nicotine affects almost every system in the body. When you take a puff, your heartbeats faster, your pulse quickens, your veins constrict, your blood pressure increases. Your adrenal glands pump out adrenaline that increases your heart rate, relaxes many of your smooth muscles, and raises your metabolic rate. Even the electrical activity in your brain changes.

These are powerful biological effects. Indeed, nicotine is a very powerful drug. In fact, it is one of the most toxic of all drugs, comparable to cyanide. Take enough nicotine and it can kill you. But the amount of nicotine in a single cigarette is only 8 to 9 milligrams on average.

The amount of nicotine that smokers inhale from each cigarette is even smaller. Most popular brands of cigarettes deliver less than 1.5 milligrams per cigarette.

This amount may be somewhat higher or lower for each smoker, depending on how deeply you puff and how many puffs you take from each cigarette.

But nicotine is so potent that even this small dose causes significant changes in the functioning of numerous organs and systems in your body. When people first take up smoking, these physiological changes seem extremely unpleasant.

Beginning smokers usually experience nausea, dizziness, headache, stomach upset, coughing and other uncomfortable symptoms. But people who continue to smoke soon develop a tolerance to these symptoms, until they become unnoticeable.

Tolerance is a term used to describe an important feature of addiction. Tolerance has developed when, after the repeated administration of a drug (in this case, nicotine) produces a decreased effect. As well, tolerance has developed when increasingly larger doses must be administered to obtain the effects observed with the original dose.

What does this mean for the smoker? The small dose of nicotine delivered by several puffs on a cigarette may make people feel ill the first few times they try smoking. But after they've been smoking for a week or so (repeated "self-administration" of nicotine), several puffs and even an entire cigarette no longer have that effect.

Psychologically, tolerance to the unpleasant effects of nicotine allows the smoker to focus on nicotine's pleasurable physiological effects.

Many smokers don't realize that nicotine's effects on the heart, the nervous system, and the endocrine system are significant contributors to the relaxation, alertness, stress relief, and other good feelings they experience.

This combination of physiological and psychological effects provides so many positive reinforcements that smoking quickly becomes an established habit.

As the term tolerance implies, a smoker actually becomes accustomed to having a certain level of nicotine in his or her body. In fact, research studies have shown that (without realizing it) smokers regulate the number of cigarettes they smoke in order to maintain their own personally preferred level of nicotine. For example, smokers who are given a very high nicotine cigarette will puff less often than usual, so they don't take in more nicotine than their preferred amount.

Likewise, with a low nicotine cigarette, the smoker will take more puffs than usual, in order to get that preferred amount of nicotine.

When no cigarettes are smoked for a while (when someone is trying to quit), the smoker doesn't get any nicotine. And it is the lack of nicotine that produces unpleasant physiological symptoms in the body. Medically, these symptoms are called "withdrawal effects."

To relieve these withdrawal effects, many smokers must continue to take in their usual amount of nicotine. This is a sign of "physical dependence" on nicotine.

Doctors define physical dependence as a change in the body's functioning that is produced by repeated administration of a drug, such that continued doses of the drug are needed to prevent withdrawal symptoms.

But that's not all. Smokers also become accustomed to the psychological effects of smoking. After the smoking habit is established, the smoker needs to smoke in to feel "normal."

In other words, the effects produced by nicotine, and the behaviors associated with smoking, become necessary to maintain the person's optimal state of well-being. This condition is referred to as "psychological dependence."

At the extreme, many smokers who run out of cigarettes or are unable to smoke, become totally preoccupied by thoughts of having a cigarette. This behavior is often referred to as "compulsive drug use."

Is Smoking An Addiction?

Physiological and physical dependence, withdrawal, and compulsive drug use are the defining characteristics of "drug addiction." Does this mean that smoking is an addiction?

Certainly, the smoking habit meets many of the criteria needed to qualify as an addiction, including:

1) A highly controlled or compulsive pattern of drug use. The experienced smoker has a lot of smoking patterns that (if broken) are disturbing.

2) Psychoactive, or mood-altering effects involved in the pattern of drug taking.

3) Drug functioning as reinforcement to strengthen behavior and lead to further drug ingestion. It's the nicotine that keeps people smoking.

Using these criteria, the U.S. Surgeon General's Report (in 1988) on smoking made several major conclusions:

• Cigarettes and other forms of tobacco are addicting.
• Nicotine is the drug in tobacco that causes addiction.
• The pharmacological and behavioral processes that determine tobacco addiction are similar to those that determine addiction to drugs such as heroin and cocaine.

All smokers show signs of physical and psychological dependence on nicotine. Their bodies crave nicotine, and they will smoke until their bodies have taken in a certain level of nicotine. Thus, addiction is more a matter of degree. Its not if you are addicted but how addicted you are.

Triggering The Habit

It's important to remember that smoking is both a habit and an addiction. There are many times when you tell yourself you're going to have a cigarette, but often, the smoking you do is just out of habit.

Your environment affects habits. Something you see or do in your daily life (a cue or a trigger) gets them going. Triggers are the stimuli associated with smoking.

What are smoking triggers? Think back to when you had just started to smoke. At first you're only positive reinforcement might have been social acceptance by your friend, that reward helped to fight against the initial negative consequences—nausea, bad taste in your mouth, tearing eyes, and burning throat.

The more you smoked, the less you were bothered by the physical discomfort. And almost without realizing it, you quickly began to enjoy smoking for many new reasons:

• You often smoked during the happy times you spent with friends.

As a result, you're now likely to smoke whenever you want to feel happier.

• You found that you ate less when you smoked, and that's helped you to control your weight. As a result, you now light a cigarette whenever you feel hungry but don't want to eat. You may even smoke between courses at a meal.

• Phone calls from your family members may sometimes be stressful. When they call, you frequently light up a cigarette to help yourself stay calm. Now you find yourself reaching for a smoke whenever you make a phone call or answer the phone, no matter who's on the line.

• If you're alone and have nothing to do, you tend to think about your worries and anxieties.

You've found that smoking relaxes you and makes you feel happier.

Cigarettes have become like "a friend" to you. In fact, you realize that you smoke the most when no friends are around and you're feeling lonely, worried, sad, or just bored.

People often say cigarettes are a "crutch" because smokers lean on their cigarettes for help in so many situations—being with friends, eating, talking on the phone, or just feeling bored.

Triggers can be any number of things, bad and good. And different smokers have different triggers.

You may connect a cigarette so strongly with a particular activity that you'd have trouble carrying out that activity without a cigarette.

For instance, some smokers always smoke when they have a cup of coffee. Other smokers can't go to sleep until they've had that last cigarette of the night. Nicotine addiction is the reason.

The physiological effects of nicotine combine with the effects of your morning coffee to give you the extra stimulation you need to get going.

Similarly, the negative feelings that nicotine counteracts (feeling sad, anxious, stressed out) all evoke strong urges for a cigarette. So you have a cigarette at bedtime, you feel more relaxed, and you're able to fall asleep.

The Three Big Reasons for Smoking

1. Nicotine is a powerful reinforcer.

2. The act of smoking offers many positive reinforcements.

3. The reinforcement becomes associated with many cues and activities in daily life.

So, smoking becomes tied to many satisfactions each day.

As you can see, triggers tend to expand and make new connections. By the time most smokers have bought this book, they may feel that almost everything they do has become a trigger for smoking. This may be true, but as you will see later, an important part of getting ready to quit is breaking up some of your strongest smoking triggers.

Smoking Is More Than Just Puffing

The process of smoking also involves buying cigarettes, removing each cigarette from the pack, lighting it, locating and handling an ashtray, blowing the smoke out of your mouth and nose, watching the smoke rise in the air, feeling the cigarette in your hand, flicking off the ashes, stubbing it out when you're finished, among many other things. In a sense, these too become triggers—the sight of the ashtray, for example.

The steps in smoking—from pouring the cup of coffee to lighting up, to stubbing it out when done—all of these become woven into a highly organized pattern that's repeated each time you smoke.

Each individual action becomes reinforced through its connection to the others in the pattern, and the eventual nicotine to which they lead. The entire array of behaviors soon takes its place as an integral part of your daily life.

Just as a person who's recently retired from a job complains that "I don't know what to do with myself," it's no wonder that people who try to quit smoking complain, "Smoking is almost constantly on my mind," and worry that they'll be unable to do without it. The cues and triggers are everywhere.

Your own personal smoking triggers—how often they occur and how strong they are—are what determine your smoking habit pattern.

Numerous research studies indicate that the single most helpful thing you can do to break the smoking habit is to take it off automatic pilot; to stop and notice your smoking triggers.

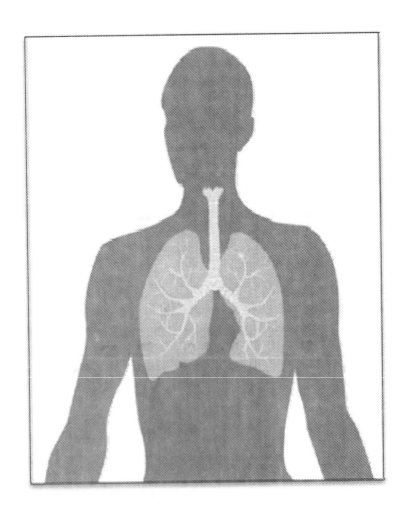

# CLEARING THE AIR ON HARD FACTS— WHAT SMOKING DOES TO YOUR BODY

Smoking is a major health hazard. There is now an exhaustive body of evidence—including hundreds of epidemiological, experimental, pathological, and clinical studies—to demonstrate that smoking increases the smoker's risk of death and illness from a wide variety of diseases. The U.S. Surgeon General has called cigarette smoking "the chief preventable cause of death in our society." The National Institute on Drug Abuse has estimated that in the U.S. alone, smoking is responsible for approximately 350,000 deaths per year.

Most smokers accept the fact that smoking is harmful, but many think of this risk as something like a game of roulette: They believe that each cigarette they smoke is like placing a bet. The "prize" is a heart attack, lung cancer, or some other disease. If your "number' comes up, you've had it, but if you are "lucky" and your number never comes up, you may avoid the hazardous effects of smoking altogether and live to a ripe old age totally unaffected by your smoking habit.

This is a serious misconception. Every cigarette you smoke harms your body. Here's a better analogy:

Suppose you lived near a chemical plant that emitted a number of toxic wastes that had seeped into the town's drinking water, so that every time you took a drink of water, it did a small amount of damage to your body. After you'd lived there for a few years, you might notice that you didn't have quite as much energy as you used to. And after five or ten years, you might notice that quite a few of the townspeople seemed to be getting ill with one thing or another.

In the same way, every cigarette you smoke damages your body. The more you smoke, the greater the damage. True, there have been people who lived into their seventies and eighties even though they smoked all their lives, but unless they were either extremely light smokers or did not inhale, they almost certainly suffered substantial physical impairment as the result of their smoking while they were alive. If they had not smoked, they would in all likelihood have lived longer.

Smoking Risks—Rules of Thumb

• Lung cancer risk—increases roughly 50 to 100 percent for each cigarette you smoke per day.
• Heart disease risks—increases roughly 100 percent for each pack of cigarettes you smoke per day.
• Switching to filter-tip cigarettes reduces the risk of lung cancer roughly 20 percent, but does not affect the risk of heart disease.
• Smokers spend 27 percent more time in the hospital and more than twice as much time in intensive care units as nonsmokers.
• Each cigarette costs the smoker five to twenty minutes of life.
• A smoker is at twice the risk of dying before age sixty-five as a nonsmoker.

Inside a Smoker's Body

Let's take a look at what happens inside your body each time you light up. You may be surprised to learn how quickly tobacco smoke can produce harmful effects.

Eyes, Nose, Throat

• Within a few seconds of your first puff, irritating gases (formaldehyde, ammonia, hydrogen sulfide, and others) begin to work on sensitive membranes of your eyes, nose, and throat. They make your eyes water and your nose run.

They irritate your throat. If you continue smoking, these irritating gases will eventually produce a smoker's cough. One of the reasons many smokers prefer menthol cigarettes is that menthol is an anesthetic that masks the smoker's perception of this irritation.

• Continued smoking produces abnormal thickening in the membranes lining your throat. This thickening is accompanied by cellular changes that have been linked to throat cancer.

Why Smokers Frequently Experience a Morning Cough

Because you haven't smoked all night, the cilia in your bronchi, which were knocked out of action by the toxic effects of cigarette smoke the day before, begin to come to life and attempt to clear the accumulated mucus out of your air passages.

This cleansing action brings up thick yellow or yellow-green mucus, which triggers the cough reflex in the back of your throat.

Lungs

• From your very first puff, the smoke begins to chip away at your lung's natural defenses. Continued exposure can completely paralyze the lungs' natural cleansing process.
• Your respiratory rate increases, forcing your lungs to work harder.
• Irritating gases produce chemical injury to the tissues of your lungs and the airways leading to the lungs.

This speeds up the production of mucus and leads to an increased tendency to cough up sputum.

• This excess mucus serves as a breeding ground for a wide variety of bacteria and viruses. This makes you more susceptible to colds, flu, bronchitis, and other respiratory infections.

And if you do come down with an infection, your body will be less able to fight it, because smoking impairs the ability of the white blood cells to resist invading organisms.

• The lining of your bronchi begins to thicken, predisposing you to cancers of the bronchi. Most lung cancers arise in the bronchial lining.
• Farther down, inside your lungs, the smoke weakens the free-roving scavenger cells that remove foreign particles from the air sacs of the lungs. Continued smoke exposure adversely affects elastin (the enzyme that keeps your lungs flexible), predisposing you to emphysema.
• Many of the compounds you inhale are deposited as a layer of sticky tar on the lining of your throat and bronchi and in the delicate air sacs of your lungs. A pack-a-day smoker pours about eight ounces—the one full cup—of tar into his or her lungs each year. This tar is rich in cancer-producing chemicals, including radioactive polonium 210.

Experiment: Breathe in a full mouthful of smoke, but don't inhale. Blow the smoke out through a clean white handkerchief is roughly equivalent to the amount each puff leaves in your lungs.

Heart

• From the moment smoke reaches your lungs, your heart is forced to work harder. Your pulse quickens, forcing your heart to beat an extra 10 to 25 times per minute, as many as 36,000 additional times per day.
• Because of the irritating effect of nicotine and other components of tobacco smoke, your heartbeat is more likely to be irregular. This can contribute to cardiac arrhythmia, and many other serious coronary conditions, such as heart attack. A recent Surgeon General's report estimated that smoking causes about 170,000 heart attacks each year.

Blood Vessels

• Your blood pressure increases by 10 to 15 percent, putting additional stress on your heart and blood vessels, increasing your risk of heart attack and stroke.
• Smoking increases your risk of vascular disease of the extremities. Severe cases may require amputation. This condition can produce pain and can increase your risk of blood clots in the lungs.

Skin

• Smoking constricts the blood vessels in your skin, decreasing the delivery of life-giving oxygen to this vital organ. As the result of this decrease in blood flow, a smoker's skin becomes more susceptible to wrinkling. This decreased blood flow can be a special problem in people who suffer from chronically cold hands and/or feet (Raynaud's Syndrome).
• Smokers are at particularly high risk for a medical syndrome called "smoker's face," which is characterized by deep lines around the corners of the mouth and eyes, a gauntness of facial features, a grayish appearance of the skin, and certain abnormalities of the complexion. In one study, 46 percent of long-term smokers were found to have smoker's face.

Blood

• Carbon monoxide—the colorless, odorless, deadly gas present in automobile exhaust—is present in cigarette smoke in more than 600 times the concentration considered safe in industrial plants. A smoker's blood typically contains 4 to 15 times as much carbon monoxide as that of a nonsmoker. This carbon monoxide stays in the bloodstream for up to six hours after you stop smoking. A 1982 University of Pittsburgh health survey found that nearly 80 percent of cigarette smokers had potentially hazardous levels of carbon monoxide in their blood.

Research suggests that these abnormally high carbon monoxide levels may play a major role in triggering heart attacks.

• When you breathe in a lung-full of cigarette smoke, the carbon monoxide passes immediately into your blood, binding to the oxygen receptor sites and figuratively kicking the oxygen molecules out of your red blood cells.

Hemoglobin that is bound to carbon monoxide is converted into carboxyhemoglobin, and is no longer able to transport oxygen. This means that less oxygen reaches a smoker's brain and other vital organs. Because of this added carbon monoxide load, a smoker's red cells are also less effective in removing carbon dioxide—a waste product—from his or her body's cells.

• If you continue to smoke for several weeks, your number of red cells begins to increase, as your body responds to chronic oxygen deprivation. This condition, characterized by an abnormally high level of red blood cells, is known as smoker's polycythemia. In addition, smoking makes your blood clot more easily. Both of these factors may increase your risk of heart attack or stroke.

Male Reproductive System

• Two recent studies by Dr. Irving Goldstein and colleagues at the New England male Reproductive Health Center, Boston University Medical School, found a possible link between smoking and erection problems. In the first study, the researchers found that among a population of 1,011 men with erection problems, 78 percent were smokers—more than twice the number of men with erection problems found in the general population.

The researchers concluded that decreased potency might result from the negative effects of smoking on the blood vessels leading to the male reproductive organs.

• In their second study, the researchers measured the blood flow to the penis in 120 men who had come to their clinic with erection problems. They found that decrease in blood flow was proportional to the number of cigarettes smoked. Dr. Goldstein believes that smoking is the leading cause of impotence in the U.S. today.

• In addition to diminishing potency, smoking adversely affects the fertility of male smokers by decreasing sperm count and sperm motility as well as altering sperm shape.

Female Reproductive System

• Women who smoke heavily show a 43 percent decline in fertility. Women smokers are three times more likely than nonsmokers to be infertile. Women who smoke also have fewer reproductive years: They reach menopause an average of 1 ¾ years earlier than nonsmokers.

Smokers' Bodies Get Less Oxygen

Because carbon monoxide lowers your blood oxygen carrying capacity, the blood delivers less oxygen to all the organs of the body. At the cellular level, oxygen is used to supply organs with the energy they need. Less oxygen means less energy.

In addition, more than thirty cancer-causing chemicals travel via the smoker's bloodstream to every organ of the body. The organs most sensitive to these carcinogens are the stomach, the kidneys, the bladder, and the cervix.

Cigarette smoking also weakens the immune system by depressing antibody response and depressing cell-mediated reactions to foreign invaders. As a result, smokers are more susceptible to a variety of infections. These impairments are reversible if the smoker stops smoking.

## Why Smoking makes You Less Fit

Although a smoker's blood carries less oxygen, the nicotine in tobacco smoke increases the heart rate, requiring more oxygen. This is why smokers become short of breath more easily than nonsmokers. The high concentration of carbon monoxide also reduces the level of oxygen that is carried to the brain. This can produce lethargy, confusion, and difficulty in thinking.

## Smoking Impairs Taste and Smell

Continued smoking will also result in a loss of your senses of taste and smell. This occurs so gradually that it may go unnoticed, but the end result is the decreased sensitivity of two very important sense perceptions.

## Smokers Die Young

In addition to producing the short-term damage described above, smoking dramatically increases the risk of illness and death. Eight major studies (involving over 2 million people) have all found that smokers die sooner than nonsmokers. The average increase in death rate among smokers was 61% overall. For smokers in the two most vulnerable age groups (35 to 45 and 45 to 55) the death rates were 86% and 152% higher.

This means that the average nonsmoker lives more than eight years longer than the average heavy smoker. Here is what smokers lose in years:

• Light Smokers give up 4.6 years of life in exchange for smoking.
• Moderate Smokers give up 5.5 years of life.
• Heavy Smokers give up 6.2 years.
• Very heavy Smokers give up 8.3 years.

Below are some figures that show the portion of deaths attributed to smoking:

Lung Cancer 85% - 90%
Bronchitis & Emphysema 85%
Mouth Cancers 70%
Throat Cancer 50%
Bladder Cancer 30% - 50%
Esophagus Cancer 20% - 40%
Pancreas Cancer 35%
Arteriosclerosis 33%
Heart Disease 30%
Kidney Disease 15% - 25%

Smokers Have More Illnesses

In addition to dying younger; smokers have increased rates of both acute and chronic illnesses. The U.S. Public Health Service has estimated that cigarettes are responsible for:

• 81 million missed days of work per year
• 145 million days spent ill in bed every year
• 11 million additional cases of chronic illness per year
• 280,000 additional cases of heart disease
• 1 million additional cases of chronic bronchitis and emphysema
• 1.8 million additional cases of chronic sinus problems
• 1 million additional cases of peptic ulcer

Compared to nonsmokers, smokers have higher rates of disease, emphysema, chronic bronchitis, peptic ulcer, allergies, and impairments of the immune system.

Pregnant women who smoke have more stillbirths and babies of reduced birth weight and children of smoking mothers are more likely to have continued difficulty developing physically and even socially throughout their lives.

Lung and Other Cancers

Cancer is a term used to describe the abnormal growth of cells that may result in the destruction of healthy tissue. Persons exposed to certain environmental carcinogens are at increased risk of some cancers. Smokers who inhale tobacco have been found to be at substantially increased risk for lung cancer. They are also at higher risk for cancers of the larynx, mouth, esophagus, bladder, kidney, and pancreas.

Smoking is the principal cause of the massive rise in death rates from lung cancer over the past 40 years. The U.S. Public Health Service estimates that smoking causes 85% to 90% of all U.S. lung cancers. The risk of lung cancer increases with the number of cigarettes smoked, how deep you inhale, and the tar content of the cigarettes you smoke.

The age at which you began smoking is also a major factor in the development of lung cancer. Males who started smoking before the age of fifteen have nearly four times the rate of lung cancer as those who began smoking after age 25. The cancer-producing effects of smoking are not seen for many years. It usually takes at least 15 to 20 years of smoking to produce lung cancer in a human.

For those smokers who are able to quit, the risk of lung cancer begins to decrease immediately. It continues to drop for the next 10 to 15 years, when it reaches a point only slightly higher than the risk for nonsmokers.

## Cardiovascular Disease

The effects of smoking on the heart and blood include increased blood clotting, an increased level of catecholamines, increased heart rate, decreased oxygen supply to the heart muscle, increased irritability of the electrical conducting system of the heart, and increased blood pressure. As a result, a smoker risk of heart disease, stroke, and other vascular abnormalities is, on average, about twice that for nonsmokers. The severity of heart attacks among smokers tends to be proportional to the cumulative dose of tobacco smoke they have inhaled in their entire smoking lives.

## Other Diseases and Conditions

1) Emphysema: Virtually everyone with emphysema gets it as the result of smoking. Smokers are also at increased risk for chronic cough, respiratory infections, and audible abnormalities in the lungs.

2) Osteoporosis: Smokers are at increased risk of thinning of bones. The bone fractures that result from loss of bone tissue are a major health problem, especially among post-menopausal women, and both men and women over 70. Researchers at the Mayo Clinic recently estimated that osteoporosis is responsible for 1.2 million fractures in the U.S. every year. Many of these fractures are fatal. Survivors frequently require long term nursing home care.

3) Smokers experience more respiratory complications during surgery.

4) A recent National Cancer Institute study showed that women who smoke have one-and-one-half-fold risk of invasive cervical cancer. Women who smoke 40 or more cigarettes per day had a two-fold risk. Those who smoke unfiltered cigarettes are at a particularly high risk.

5) Smokers are at increased risk of cancers of the larynx, mouth, esophagus, bladder, pancreas, kidney, and stomach.

6) Smokers are at increased risk for both peptic and duodenal ulcers.

7) Smokers are at increased risk of gum disease.

8) Recent studies suggest that smokers may be at four-fold risk of developing Alzheimer's disease.

9) Smokers are at increased risk of being hurt or killed in house fires (as are all people who live with or near them). Some 39% of the people killed in fires caused by negligent use of cigarettes were not the smokers involved.

Effects of Tobacco Smoke on Nonsmokers

Nonsmokers exposed to smoke-filled rooms show carbon monoxide blood levels equivalent to those of light smokers. Among adults exposed to tobacco smoke, the most common symptoms are eye irritation, headaches, nasal irritation, and cough. Exposure to smoke can also trigger or aggravate allergic symptoms. Respiratory illness is more common in children exposed to tobacco smoke. And there is now considerable evidence to suggest that passive smoking may increase the risk of both heart attacks and lung cancer among the nonsmokers.

Effects of Cutting Down and Quitting

The good news for smokers is that the great majority of negative health effects caused by smoking are dose-related. That is to say, the risk is proportional to the number of particles that pass into the body. Thus every step you can take to reduce the risk of your "dose" of tobacco smoke will help improve your health.

## WHAT TYPE OF SMOKER ARE YOU?

Because of the way newspapers, radio, and TV deal with risk, it's difficult for us to understand the relative importance of the various risks in our lives. We read newspaper headlines about products that have been taken off the market because consuming them might lead to a one-in-a-million chance of getting cancer.

Many smokers quite understandably feel that if cigarettes really posed a substantial health risk, they would hear more about it than they presently do. Unfortunately, this is not the case.

### 1,475 Deaths Per Day

If three commercial 747 jumbo jets were to crash every day for an entire year, it would certainly make front-page news and deservedly so, for this would add up to about 540,000 deaths per year. But according to one current estimate, the number of premature deaths caused or accelerated by cigarette smoking works out to the same number. This adds up to 1,475 deaths per day. Other experts have estimated the number of excess deaths at 350,000 per year, "merely" 1,000 excess deaths per day.

If you knew that three jumbo jets would go down in flames today, you would probably be extremely wary about boarding a commercial airliner. Yet 54 million smokers light up every day, most of them without a second thought.

### What makes a "Tragedy"?

The risk of dying in a plane crash and the risk of smoking related disease are treated quite differently for a number of reasons:

31

Unexpected, surprising news triggers terror and fear, while the "same old story" has lost its news value and is easily ignored. Furthermore, when misfortune befalls a large group of people together, it is perceived as much more "tragic" than if the same numbers of individuals were to suffer a similar fate individually. Thus, if a bus containing sixty people is involved in a traffic accident and all occupants are killed, this is considered a much more important "tragedy" than if sixty motorists were to die in sixty separate accidents.

## Voluntary vs. Involuntary Risks

In addition to the factors above, people will accept risks that are substantially higher—as much as 100 times higher—if they are able to choose such activities freely. People don't like to be forced to accept risks—even though they might choose to take similar or greater risks in other matters. This helps explain the unwillingness of nonsmokers to accept even the relatively small risks of "passive" smoking—because they are forced to breathe tobacco smoke against their will.

Some smokers console themselves that although smoking may indeed be dangerous, they could just as easily be murdered on the street or die in an auto accident. But a review of the facts makes it clear that this is little more than a convenient self-deception. Of every 1,000 young male smokers, one will be murdered, six will die on the roads, and tobacco related diseases would kill 250.

## Average Risks vs. Actual Risks

The smoking-related risks of heart disease, cancer, and other diseases are already discussed in the previous chapter. But these are all average risks. Some smokers are at even higher risk of being injured or killed by smoking.

You may be at increased risk if:

• You have a medical condition that is made worse by smoking;
• You have an inherited susceptibility to a smoking related disease;
• You are exposed to environmental or occupational toxins;
• You are an especially heavy smoker;
• Psychological or social factors might make it especially difficult for you to quit, even if you should decide to do so.

Risk is Proportional to Total Lifetime Dose

When a physician or other health professional takes a complete medical history, one item that is always included, for smokers, is the Total Lifetime Dose (TLD) of tobacco smoke.

The TLD, usually expressed in pack-years, is a rough approximation of the number of cigarettes you have consumed over your lifetime. One pack-year equals 365 packs or 7,300 cigarettes. Since patterns of inhalation vary widely from smoker to smoker, a pack–year is a relatively rough measure.

Two smokers' actual effective dose of tar, carbon monoxide, and nicotine may vary considerably, even though they may have smoked the same number of cigarettes over their lifetime:

• Those who smoke low-tar brands may be exposed to less tar (though not necessarily less carbon monoxide) than those who smoke unfiltered, high-tar brands.
• Those who take more puffs per cigarette are at greater risk than those who take fewer puffs.
• Those who smoke their cigarette farther down, leaving shorter butts, are at greater risk than those who extinguish their cigarette earlier.

• Those who inhale deeply are at greater risk than those who inhale little or no smoke.

With these qualifications, the factor that seems to be proportional to risk is your total lifetime dose (TLD)--the total number of cigarettes you have smoked since your very first cigarette.

## Calculating Your Lifetime Dose

Your total lifetime dose is proportional to the average number of cigarettes smoked per day times the number of years you have smoked.

This number is relatively easy to calculate:

1. Determine the number of years you have smoked.

2. Determine the approximate number of packs you smoked per day for each year.

3. Add up the pack-year figures to get your lifetime smoking dose.

Your health risk is roughly proportional to your total lifetime dose. The greater your lifetime dose, the greater your risk of coming down with a smoking-related disease. Thus, if you have smoked three packs a day for fifty years, you would have a TLD of 150. If you have smoked ten cigarettes per day for four years, you would have a TLD of 2.

## Ten Types of High-Risk Smokers

The sections that follow outline ten risk factors than can make some individuals more vulnerable to smoking-related injury or disease. These high-risk categories are as follows:

1. Pregnant women.
2. Women over thirty who take birth control pills.
3. Members of families at high risk for heart disease.

4. Smokers who already have smoking-related diseases.
5. Smokers exposed to toxic agents in the workplace.
6. Smokers with high-risk lifestyles.
7. Smokers with high-risk personalities.
8. Smokers about to undergo surgery.
9. Smokers with abnormal lab tests or family histories.
10. Smokers who are heavily addicted to nicotine.

## 1. Pregnant Women

The babies of women who smoke suffer from a variety of negative consequences, including lower birth weight, shorter stature, smaller head and arm circumferences, and higher risk of prematurity, higher risk of spontaneous abortion, decreased fetal movements, increased risk of early rupture of fetal membranes, and higher risk of neurological impairment when compared to the babies of nonsmokers. The decrease in birth weight is greatest if the mother is a heavy smoker.

Maternal smoking has negative effects on the baby's breathing; moreover, the baby's heart rate increases as soon as its mother lights up a cigarette. Overall, the risk of death during or before birth is 27 percent higher for the babies of smoking mothers.

Smoking slows the baby's growth through two independent pathways:

• Carbon monoxide poisoning—Carbon monoxide passes freely from the mother's circulatory system into the baby's bloodstream and tissues, decreasing the baby's available oxygen levels.
• Increased catecholamine levels—Nicotine increases the release of catecholamines, hormones that narrow the baby's arteries and limit blood flow.

Most researchers would now agree that prospective mothers who smoke during pregnancy might well be committing inadvertent child abuse.

If there is one group of smokers who should most definitely quit smoking – it is pregnant women.

If all efforts fail at quitting, pregnant women should at the very least:

1) Reduce their smoking to five or less low-tar cigarettes per day.

2) Supplement their diet with extra portions of milk, eggs, and cheese during their pregnancy.

It is now a well-established fact that reduction of smoking during pregnancy improves the birth weight of the infant. Quitting smoking altogether during pregnancy provides optimal conditions for fetal growth.

2. Women Over Thirty Who Take Birth Control Pills

Mixing cigarettes and birth control can lead to heart attack and stroke. Risks are particularly high for smokers over 40.

The risks are higher for women who smoke more than 25 cigarettes per day. Women under 35 can take the Pill without increasing their risk to dangerous levels – provided they do not smoke.

Women over 40 who do not smoke should take the Pill only in extreme situations. Smokers over 30 who are on the Pill and are unable to quit should switch to another form of birth control.

3. Members of Families At High Risk for Heart Disease

Have any of your close relatives died of heart disease before age 45?

If they have, and you smoke, you have three times the normal risk of developing smoking-related heart disease.

## 4. Smokers Who Already Have Smoking-Related Diseases

Such diseases include heart disease, lung cancer, emphysema, chronic bronchitis, ulcers, high blood pressure, diabetes, osteoporosis, blood clots in the legs, and glaucoma.

## 5. Smokers Exposed to Toxic Agents in the Workplace

No chemical or industrial by-product comes close to equaling tobacco smoke as a health hazard. Researchers estimate that smoking 1.4 cigarettes produces a risk of loss of life comparable to consuming 100 charcoal-broiled steaks or living near to a polyvinyl-chloride (PVC) plant for 20 years.

The categories of workers listed below may be exposed to toxic substances that combine with tobacco smoke to put smokers at a significantly greater risk than nonsmokers exposed to these same substances:

• Workers exposed to carbon monoxide (firefighters, traffic control officers, traffic police, bus drivers, tunnel workers, turnpike workers).
• Workers exposed to asbestos. Asbestos workers who smoke may be at 50 times risk of lung disease compared to nonsmokers not exposed to asbestos.
• Workers exposed to sulfur dioxide, uranium, coal and coal dust, cotton dust, mineral dusts, and other particulate matter (silica, mica, iron oxide, aluminum oxide) show small airway damage similar to that suffered by asbestos workers. They may be at similar risk for lung disease.•
Quarry workers, mine workers, grain workers, forestry workers, woodworkers, construction workers, iron and steel foundry workers, aluminum workers, shipyard workers, car industry workers, rubber workers, hospital workers exposed

to high levels of ethylene oxide (a chemical used to sterilize surgical instruments).

• Workers exposed to arsenic, beryllium, chloromethyl ethers, chromium, radiation, mustard gas, or nickel, and those who worked in factories manufacturing polyvinylchloride before 1975.

6. Smokers With High-Risk Lifestyles

Current research suggests that the following groups of smokers are at increased risk from smoking and/or are much more likely to smoke:

• People who are overweight, especially those with substantial fat deposits in their abdomens, in other words a big gut. Here's the easiest way to find out whether you are at risk for both heart attack and stroke: Take your waist and hip measurements, and then divide your waist measurement by your hip measurement. A ratio of more than 1.0 in men or 0.8 in women suggests that you may be at increased risk.

• People who are extremely thin.
• Heavy drinkers.
• People who are unmarried, divorced, or separated.
• Lack of exercise.

7. Smokers With High-Risk Personalities

Research has shown that smokers have different personalities than nonsmokers. Smokers tend to be more extroverted, defiant, and impulsive. They are more likely to take risks and more likely to be divorced or separated. They consume more alcohol, coffee, psychoactive drugs, and aspirin than nonsmokers.

## 8. Smokers About to Undergo Surgery

Studies show that complications during surgery are as much as 2.4 times higher in smokers. This effect can be considerably reversed by a mere 12 hours without cigarettes.

The principal culprit is carbon monoxide. Smoking reduces the oxygen-carrying capacity of your blood. This is especially dangerous during anesthesia.

## 9. Smokers with Abnormal Lab Tests or Family Histories

The following risk factors may significantly increase your smoking risks:

• A family history of high blood pressure.
• High serum cholesterol.
• Emphysema.
• High heart rate.
• Abnormal EKG (also called ECG: electrocardiograph).
• High hematocrit. The hematocrit measures the percentage of blood volume that is made up of red blood cells.

## 10. Smokers Who Are Heavily Addicted to Nicotine

Persons who are strongly addicted to nicotine are usually heavier smokers and tend to have a more difficult time cutting down or quitting because of their extreme degree of nicotine dependence.

One key sign of being heavily addicted needs a cigarette immediately after waking up. The number of minutes between waking up and lighting the first cigarette of the day appears to be a useful index of addiction.

Other signs of intense addiction are:

• Experiencing the first cigarette of the day as the most satisfying.

• Smoking heavily first thing in the morning.

• Having difficulty refraining from smoking in no-smoking areas.

• Smoking more than 25 cigarettes per day.

• Being unable to cut down or quit when you are ill.

• Smoking high-nicotine or unfiltered cigarettes.
• Inhaling deeply on every puff.

• Smoking each cigarette down to a short butt.

• Lighting a new cigarette right after finishing the last one.

• Experiencing severe anxiety about running out of cigarettes.

## WHAT YOU NEED TO HELP YOU QUIT

Now that you understand the dangers that smoking brings about, you need to start making plans to quit. The first step is adopting a healthier lifestyle, which includes eating right, exercising, managing stress and getting support from family and friends.

Taking these pro-health steps is your valuable first step towards quitting, since it will prepare you psychologically to make a firm commitment to quitting.

A healthier lifestyle is a no-lose proposition. And these lifestyle measures will certainly affect other areas of your life.

First of all, keep in mind that three out of four smokers would like to quit. Five out of six say they would not start smoking in the first place, if they had the choice to make over again. In fact, most smokers eventually do quit smoking.

The 1989 Surgeon General's Report estimated that almost 50% of all adults who had ever smoked regularly had quit.

But quitting smoking isn't easy. Studies have shown that many successful quitters failed in their first attempts to quit. There's actually little connection between the number of previous quit attempts and eventual success. So previous failures do not mean that you can't succeed.

Quitting smoking is hard to do. It requires strong motivation.

Motivations don't just happen. You have to take an active part in developing your motivations and making them more effective.

STEP 1:

To start off, think about how you think about quitting. Do you think of it as giving something up? Instead, try thinking of it as a positive act – improving your health, taking control of your life.

It will help you to believe it is possible for you to quit. If you have quit before, try reframing your past "failure" as a success. First of all, you were able to quit for some length of time (probably for longer than you thought you could). You learned some things that will help you this time. You probably learned you can't "just have one." And maybe you recognized some triggers or temptations you really need to watch out for.

As we have seen, there are many reasons why you smoke – habit, addition, social enjoyment, stress relief, hunger control, advertising messages, and more. In fact, your reasons often change from day to day. Smoking fills different needs at different times of the day.

Each time you smoke, you reinforce the connection between the act of smoking and your current activity or situation. You no longer think about needing something to do with your hands. Instead, you automatically smoke whenever you're on the telephone, or when you're waiting in line, or when you're taking a coffee break.

These feelings and situations serve as triggers – cues to light up. Think for a moment, and try to find out your personal "triggers." What are some of the triggers you have had today? What situations caused you to have a cigarette? Smoking is such an automatic habit that most people don't think about what triggers it, or how important any particular trigger is. Start acting like you can quit.

STEP 2:

Perhaps your doctor has told you to quit. Studies show that many doctors do advise smokers to quit, but in a way that's easy to ignore. If your doctor hasn't talked to you about quitting, you may think that it's not important. But it is. And often doctors are frustrated that their patients continue to smoke. When you go see a doctor, there is little time to have a long discussion about the importance of quitting, since there are other physical problems that the doctor has to deal with.

How about you? Do you have some nagging health concerns that you've tried to brush off, because you're afraid that it could be something serious? For example, many smokers have a chronic heavy cough, which often brings up mucus. Coughing is an early warning sign of potential lung damage. More severe problems such as shortness of breath, wheezing, and coughing up blood could be a sign of chronic obstructive pulmonary disease, or even lung cancer. Chest pain could be a sign of cardiovascular disease. These are serious problems that should not be ignored.

Think about other health concerns that you have. And then think about how these problems might be made worse by your smoking. This is not a very pleasant job, but when you start to learn how smoking is affecting your health, you will be motivated to quit. Examine your health concerns.

STEP 3:

Once you have faced your health concerns, you may become more aware of other reasons to stop smoking. For example, does it seem as if more and more people are asking you not to smoke? If so, you have probably realized that the anti-smoking message has spread quickly.

Most people start smoking because of social pressures (to fit in, to look older, more sophisticated, and sexier). Once they become smokers in today's world, however, they're increasingly pressured not to smoke. With this changing social climate, nonsmokers have become more aggressive about approaching total strangers and asking them to butt out.

For some people this type of pressure can be a motivation to keep smoking. But on the other hand, studies have shown that the changing norms regarding smoking behavior are also helping people to quit. Social pressures are demanding that you stop smoking.

STEP 4:

One place where important social norms can encourage non-smoking is at work. Many workplaces now sponsor quit smoking clinics. Companies have actually found that they are cost-effective because nonsmokers miss fewer days of work and make less use of medical benefits. So, quitting smoking will help you feel part of the team at work. Try to become a nonsmoker at work, or cut down.

STEP 5:

Most people who stop smoking do so out of personal reasons. This means that your own reasons for wanting to quit may be very different from someone else. Knowing your own reasons for quitting (and remembering them when things get a little tough) will be big steps in helping you become a nonsmoker for life. Find out your personal reasons. These can include:

• I will have more control of my life
• I will be healthier
• My heart rate and blood pressure will be lower
• I'll save lots of money
• I'm tired of having stinky clothes and smelly breath.

• I'll have more energy
• I'll decrease of chances of getting heart disease, chronic bronchitis, emphysema and cancer.
• Other reasons:_____

Now rank your reasons for quitting in order of importance. Next, list any reasons you can think of for NOT quitting. Once you've made your list, study it for a few minutes every day. Keep adding to it new reasons that occur to you. Make this active process each and every day.

STEP 6:

The dilemma most smokers face is that they want to quit – but they also want to keep smoking. Your reasons to be hesitant about quitting are real. Don't hide from them. Be open to thinking about both these and your reasons for quitting. Then, when you decide you really want to quit, your resolve will be stronger. You will have acknowledged that you do have valid reasons for wanting to keep smoking – it's just that your reasons for wanting to quit are stronger.

Weight your reasons for smoking and for quitting carefully. Use paper and pencil and write down the reasons why you would make either choice. Then compare them. That way you can make a clear choice between them. When people lose sight of their choices, they begin to feel deprived. And that's when negative thinking takes over. It's important for you to see that there are two choices.

But changing a behavior like smoking is as much emotional as it is rational. Smoking has nothing to do with how smart you are. You must bring together what you know in your head and your heart with your gut feeling. Then you will begin to increase your desire to quit and your confidence in your ability to do it.

STEP 7:

The fear of quitting – of never ever having a cigarette again
– makes some people leave a back window open – as an
excuse for going back to smoking. Some of these
"windows" include:

• Fear of gaining weight
• Crabbiness
• A minor relapse, so you might as well smoke
• Family quarrels
• Work pressure

Before you quit smoking, you have to close all these open
"windows." Begin by deciding what you are going to do
about each barrier and each roadblock that's holding you
back.

STEP 8:

You need two types of confidence to succeed in quitting:

• Confidence in this book, since it works for all types of
smokers and it will work for you whether you smoke a few
cigarettes a day or three packs a day.
• Confidence in yourself. You can begin building that
confidence by using a positive attitude. For starters,
practice saying out loud, "I can quit smoking!"
As you go along, make up other confidence statements. For
example, "I can stop smoking and maintain my current
weight." Or "I can stop smoking and learn new ways to
manage stress." Or "I love myself too much to let myself
smoke."

Words are often not enough. It also helps to review other
things you've done that required priority-setting and
resisting temptation. Maybe you learned how to get your
taxes done early. Maybe you lost 20 pounds and kept them
off. Maybe you developed better ways of handling
disagreements with your spouse or your children.

# DEVELOP YOUR QUITTING PLAN

There are three basic questions you have to answer in developing your personal plan to quit smoking:

1) What type of program is best for you?

• A self-help plan. If this is your choice, everything you need is in this book.
• A group support program or individual counseling to supplement the information in this book.

2) What method of quitting is best for you?

• Cold turkey. You set a quit date and when that day comes, you stop smoking entirely.
• Nicotine fading. A process of changing the type of cigarettes you smoke to gradually reduce your nicotine intake before you quit altogether.

3) Do you want to use medications to boost your effort?

Many smokers quit successfully without assistance from nicotine replacement products or drug treatment. This is a popular approach.

• Nicotine replacement. Current choices among nicotine patches, nicotine sprays, nicotine nasal sprays, and nicotine inhalers are widely available in the market.
• Medication available from your doctor can also help in quitting smoking.
• Some people have found that hypnosis and acupuncture also helps.

Each of these questions is independent of the others. You can decide on one or more choices for each. Experts have found that the most popular method of quitting is cold turkey. But you should be careful about this method, because just throwing away your cigarettes on a whim rarely works for more than a day or two. On the other hand, planning a quit date and then quitting all-or-nothing on that date always works.

Group Cessation Clinics

There's nothing more tried and proven than group smoking cessation clinics. These programs are offered by many hospitals and in many worksites, as well as by voluntary agencies such as the American Lung Association.

Smokers often wonder whether they should try quitting on their own or through a group program. There's no sure answer. But think about how you like to work. If you like to work things out for yourself (such as build furniture or home devices from books), then quitting on your own may be for you. On the other hand, if you work well in groups, and enjoy meetings, then a group program may work for you.

If you contact a group program, the representatives should be able to describe it for you and answer your questions. If they can't, move on to another program. If they give you the information you need, ask yourself if it sounds like a program that would bring out the best in you. If so, give it a try.

If you're trying to decide whether a group is right for you, here are questions to ask when you cal for information:

1) Is the program convenient? Find out where it's being held, what day and time, and how many sessions are involved.

2) Is the staff well trained and professional? Ask who will be leading the group. If a recognized educational, public health or medical organization offers the program, the staff is likely to be well qualified.

If the program involves hypnosis, the leader should be a licensed or certified professional in psychiatry, psychology, or social work.

If medications are to be used, a physician or other health professional should be involved in screening participants before treatment.

3) Does the program provide what you need? Find out whether the program emphasizes lectures or group discussions. Will you get help with controlling stress and weight gain? Does the program offer assistance after the group sessions are over?

Be wary if the staff says their program contains a special, foolproof method that will do everything for you.

4) What is the success rate of the program? Research shows that group programs are successful for about 20% to 30% of participants. With the addition of nicotine replacement products, hypnosis, and group support to stay off cigarettes, success rates may be increased.

A good program follows up on participants for at least three months. Those who are judged "successfully quit" should be reported as a percentage of all those who participated in the program at least once or twice – including those who dropped out.

5) How much will it cost? Price does not necessarily reflect the value of the program. Group programs can cost less than $50 and as much as several thousand dollars.

If your employer or health care offers a stop-smoking program, it's likely to be less expensive for you.

Nicotine Fading:

With the nicotine fading method you reduce your nicotine dose slowly over one or two weeks but stills smoke your regular number of cigarettes.

You can do this by switching brands. As you know, different brands of cigarettes provide different amounts of nicotine. By switching to cigarettes with lower levels of nicotine, you can gradually bring down your addiction to nicotine before you quit smoking. This will help you avoid a steep drop in your nicotine level that can cause strong withdrawal symptoms. You will then be able to stop smoking more easily when your quit day arrives.

If you choose this method, it is important to establish a written plan to fade. There is tendency to smoke more cigarettes when you reduce their nicotine content. Below is a list of cigarette brands according to their nicotine content:

High Nicotine
Alpine
American
Benson & Hedges
Best Buy
Best Value
Cambridge
Camel
Century 25's
Chesterfield
Convoy
Cost Cutter
Craven A
Dunhill
Eli Cutter
English Ovals
Eve Slim Lights
Famous Value
Gridlock
Harley Davidson
Herbert Tareyton
Hi-Lite

Kent 100's
Kool
L & M
Lark
Lucky Strike
Malibu
Marlboro
Max
More
Newport
Old Gold
Pall Mall
Philip Morris
Players
P.M. Blues
Richland
Salem
Spring
Stride
Tall
Tareyton Medium Nicotine
Belair
Benson & Hedges Lights
Cambridge Lights
Camel Lights
Capri
Century Lights
Cost Cutter Lights
Falcon Lights
Famous Value Lights
Fiesta
Kent Golden Lights
Kim
Kool Lights/Mild
L & M Lights
Lucky Strike Lights
Magna

Malibu Lights
Marlboro Lights
Marlboro Mediums
Merit
More Lights
Newport Lights
Newport Lights
No Frills
Old Gold Lights
Pall Mall Lights
Parliament Lights
Pyramid Ultra Lights
Raleigh Lights
Richland Lights
Ritz
Royale Lights
Salem Lights
Saratoga
Satin
Silva Thins
True 100's
Vantage
Viceroy Lights
Virginia Slims Lights
Winston Lights Low Nicotine
Benson & Hedges Ultra Lights
Bright 100's
Carlton
Cost Cutter Ultra Lights
Doral Ultra Lights
Famous Value Ultra Lights
Gridlock Ultra Lights
Merit Ultra Lights
Now
Salem Ultra Lights
Triumph
True

Vantage Ultra Lights
Virginia Slims Ultra Lights
Winston Ultra Lights

If your brand is not on the list, you can assume the following:

1) If it's an unfiltered cigarette or if it's a filtered cigarette and does not contain the words "light" or "ultra light," consider it as a high-nicotine brand.

2) If it's a filtered cigarette and contains the word "light" or "mild," assume it's a medium-nicotine brand.

3) If it's a filtered cigarette and contains the words "ultra light," assume it's a low-nicotine brand.

As you proceed with nicotine fading, it's important to remember that this is merely a temporary measure. The main benefit to your health, of course, comes from quitting entirely.

Nicotine Replacement Therapy

Before discussing this possibility is it important to remember: YOU MUST QUIT SMOKING ENTIRELY BEFORE STARTING TO USE ANY NICOTINE REPLACEMENT PRODUCT.

If you feel that you are severely addicted to cigarettes, you may wish to consider using a nicotine substitute product:

• Nicotine gum
• Nicotine patch
• Nicotine nasal spray
• Nicotine inhaler

People usually develop cravings for things that develop immediate satisfaction, such as chocolate or cigarettes.

Since nicotine replacement provides nicotine, but not the quick nicotine uptake of cigarettes, it's easier to give up nicotine replacement than it is to give up cigarettes.

With the patch, the nicotine level in your body stays relatively constant day after day. There is no immediate satisfaction, so there is less craving for a patch. As a result, "quitting" nicotine replacement after you're securely off cigarettes is generally pretty easy.

Nicotine patches, gums, inhalers, and nasal sprays are expensive. But during the first year alone, a pack-a-day smoker who successfully quits smoking will more than pay for the medication with the money saved from not buying cigarettes.

Here are some important things that you should know about nicotine replacement products:

• Nicotine patches and nicotine gum are available over-the-counter. The nicotine nasal spray and nicotine inhaler are currently available only by prescription from a doctor.
• These products provide a small amount of nicotine that will help relieve many of the withdrawal symptoms that a smoker may feel when quitting.
• The goal is to be free of both cigarettes and the nicotine substitute within three to six months.

As mentioned in the beginning of this section, you must quit smoking completely before you use any nicotine replacement.

This means that you must not smoke while using these products. If you do, you may develop serious side effects caused by an overdose of nicotine.

Pregnant or nursing women must not use nicotine replacement.

With any nicotine substitute, it's always wise to check with your doctor to see if there are medical reasons you should not use these products.

Nicotine Gum:

This is a drug in gum form, with enough nicotine to reduce your urge to smoke. The gum releases small amounts of nicotine, which is absorbed into the body through the mucous membranes of the mouth. This cuts down on withdrawal symptoms and makes it easier to break the smoking addiction. It tastes very different from regular gum, because it is a medicine.

You can buy nicotine gum from drug stores, mass merchandisers, and supermarkets. Package instructions explain how the gum is used. Most smokers chew 10 to 15 pieces of gum a day. However, you can have up to 30 pieces. It's important to use as many you need to feel comfortable without cigarettes.

Use only one piece of gum at a time. Chew it slowly very slowly until you feel a tingle in your mouth. When the peppery taste is present, shift the gum between your cheek and gum. When the tingle is gone, chew a few more times to get it back. Then shift the gum to different parts of your mouth. Repeat this procedure for about 30 minutes to release most of the nicotine.

The majority of the time, the gum should be just sitting in your mouth. Do not chew continuously and swallow the saliva as you would with regular gum.

The nicotine from the gum must be absorbed through the mouth – it is ineffective if swallowed. The nicotine does not reach the bloodstream if it goes to the stomach, and it can cause heartburn or hiccups.

Another important point is: Do not use nicotine gum while you are drinking. This will wash the nicotine down to the stomach. Wait several minutes after drinking liquid before chewing the gum. This is particularly important if you have been, or will be, drinking acidic beverages such as orange or grapefruit juice, since the acidic quality of these drinks changes the "environment" of the mouth and interferes with the amount of nicotine that's absorbed.

Begin using the gum after you quit smoking, and use it every day for at least two or three months after quitting. The first three months are when relapse is most likely to happen. Remember that you must not chew the gum and smoke cigarettes.

As your urges to smoke decrease, you will gradually reduce your use of the gum. However, there are two cautions:

1) It's better to use the gum a little longer than to risk a relapse by tapering off the gum too early and too quickly.

2) Even after you stop using the gum, continue to carry some with you just in case. Better to relapse to the gum than to cigarettes.

Nicotine Patch:

The nicotine patch is applied to your skin. Over a prolonged period of time, the nicotine dissolves right through the skin and enters the body. Nicotine from the patch replaces some of the nicotine you were getting from cigarettes.

This can relieve some of the physical symptoms associated with quitting smoking, so you can concentrate on your behavioral and psychological addiction to cigarettes.

You can buy the patch without a prescription – but as always, it's best to check with your doctor to see if the patch is right for you.

You may not be able to use the patch if:

• You are taking certain prescription medicines, or
• You have cardiovascular disease or certain other health conditions.

Even if you have been told not to use the patch because of a medical condition, you may want to check back with your doctor from time to time, to see if your condition or the medical advisories have changed. For example, physicians were initially concerned that nicotine patch use might be dangerous for cigarette smokers who have coronary artery disease. However, a recent study found that the patch is a safe way for such people to quit smoking, and may improve blood and oxygen flow to the heart. Some research has suggested that the patch is safe and effective for teenage smokers, but patch use is currently not advised for people less than 18 years of age.

The nicotine patch is safe but (as with any medication) it must be used with caution. Most important, you should never smoke while using the patch.

Some side effects from normal use of the patch can include headaches, dizziness, upset stomach, diarrhea, weakness, or blurred vision. Vivid dreams also may result from an interrupted sleep pattern when you quit smoking.

Some people report a mild itching or burning on the skin where the patch is applied, which usually goes away in about an hour. If the irritation continues you can try moving the patch to a different spot. If it persists, remove the patch and contact your doctor.

Some patches contain more nicotine than others. Some smokers start with the strongest patch. Then after several weeks, you can switch to a medium-strength patch for a few weeks, and possibly a lower-strength patch for the last few weeks. On the other hand, some people prefer the simplicity of a single-strength patch.

If you do use the nicotine patch, each morning you will apply a new nicotine patch to a clean, dry, non-hairy part of your upper body or arm. Don't apply creams on the skin where you will put the patch. Press the patch firmly on your skin. It should stick to the skin well, allowing you to do all of your usual activities, including bathing.

One brand of the nicotine patch is removed at night, lowering the level of nicotine in the bloodstream, to give the body a rest. Other brands are worn at night as well as during the daytime, and are changed once every 24 hours. When you remove the patch, put a fresh patch on a new area of your upper body. Do not reuse a skin area for at least one week.

The nicotine patch isn't magic. It can't automatically wipe out all your cravings for nicotine. Cravings are diminished and may not last with the patch, but don't expect them to disappear immediately.

Even if you still crave cigarettes sometimes while wearing the patch, you are less likely to suffer from several of the major smoking withdrawal symptoms, such as tension, irritability, feeling sleepy, and having a hard time concentrating.

Other Products:

Nicotine replacement therapy can also be administered via a nasal spray, or by the newest method, an oral inhaler, which was approved by the Food and Drug Administration in 1997.

These products are available only by prescription. Contact your doctor to see if the nicotine spray or inhaler is right for you.

As with all nicotine replacement products, you cannot start using the nasal spray and the inhaler until you have completely stopped smoking. If you do use nicotine spray or a nicotine inhaler, you must not smoke any cigarettes, or use any other form of tobacco, such as cigars, pipes, or chewing tobacco.

The spray delivers nicotine through the nose. The inhaler delivers nicotine into the mouth, which produces a sensation in the back of the throat similar to that produced by tobacco smoke. However, both devices provide nicotine at a lower level than cigarettes, and they do not contain any of the cancer-causing tars and toxins found in tobacco products. For example, ten puffs on the inhaler provides about the same amount of nicotine as one puff on an average cigarette.

With the nicotine spray and inhaler, dosage is flexible and can be individualized according to your personal withdrawal symptoms. Both devices deliver nicotine to the blood stream in a matter of minutes. This fast onset of action reduces nicotine cravings quickly. Unlike the nicotine patch, gum, and nasal spray, the nicotine inhaler has the advantage of satisfying the "hand-to-mouth" ritual smokers miss when they quit. The inhaler consists of a mouthpiece connected to a cartridge containing nicotine.

When a smoker puffs on the mouthpiece, the inhaled air becomes saturated with nicotine, which is absorbed through the mucous membranes of the mouth and throat, as happens with nicotine gum.

This route of absorption isn't the same as that of cigarettes. A majority of the nicotine from a cigarette is absorbed directly into the lungs, which causes a "nicotine spike" that smokers feel almost instantly. It's this spike a smoker gets when taking a puff or a drag that contributes to the high addictive properties of tobacco.

Is Nicotine Replacement Unhealthy?

Many people worry that nicotine replacement products are just as bad as smoking cigarettes. They're definitely not. They do not have all the tars and poisonous gases that are found in cigarettes. They provide less nicotine than a smoker would get from cigarettes. And they're designed to help people get off nicotine, not to keep them on nicotine.

But it is important to realize that nicotine replacement therapies will not work for everyone. They are not a cure-all. They are just temporary aids that can help you make it through the tough initial withdrawal period after you've quit smoking.

What needs to be understood is that nicotine is not the only dangerous element of the smoking habit. Certain moods, times of day, or activities all become strong triggers that make you crave a cigarette.

Nicotine replacement isn't a cure for these. That's why anyone who uses the nicotine patch, gum, nasal spray, inhaler, or other products should also make a concerted effort to change their behavior patterns.

The Non-Nicotine Pill:

There is a new prescription pill that's designed to help smokers quit. Again, it's still not a magic pill. It does not eliminate the urges to smoke. Those urges still require a serious effort to overcome.

The pill is Zyban, the trade-name for a sustained-release tablet of bupropion hydrochloride. The same drug has been sold under the trade-name Wellbutrin SR. Now it's being marketed as the first non-nicotine prescription treatment for smoking addiction.

How does the pill work for smokers? The drug boosts the body's levels of two "brain chemicals," dopamine and norepinephrine – the same thing happens with nicotine. Actions of these chemicals in the brain give people a sense of energy and well-being. Nicotine produces the same feelings.

According to the advertisements, using bupropion allows smokers to get the same feeling, while weaning themselves off nicotine. For many people, this helps to reduce withdrawal symptoms and lessens the urge to smoke. But like the other nicotine replacement products, the pill should be used in combination with a quit-smoking behavior modification program.

In one study, the non-nicotine pill helped more smokers to quit than the nicotine patch. Using both the pill and the patch was even more effective, but the combination poses the risk of increasing blood pressure.

Zyban is usually taken twice a day – one pill in the morning and one in the early evening. It takes about a week for the pill to reach an effective level in the body. Therefore, smokers must start taking the pill before they quit smoking. Then you set a Quit Day within one to two weeks after starting treatment. Most smokers then take the pill for a total of 7 to 12 weeks.

The non-nicotine pill is available only by prescription. It's especially important to get a doctor's advice, because

Zyban is certainly not right for everyone. The drug is not recommended for:

• Women who are pregnant or breast-feeding.
• People with a history of eating disorders, such as bulimia or anorexia nervosa.
• Anyone who is currently taking or has taken a monoamine oxidase inhibitor (MAO) medication for depression.
• People already taking Wellbutrin, Wellbutrin SR, or other medicines that contain buproprion hydrochloride.
• People who have a seizure disorder, such as epilepsy.

Seizures disorders are a special concern. Buproprion is known to cause seizures in approximately 1 out of every 1000 people taking buproprion hydrochloride. Although this is a small risk, it may be an important factor for people deciding whether or not to use this drug. Other common side effects include dry mouth and difficulty in sleeping.

The Role of Drugs in Quitting

The introduction of buproprion as an aid in smoking cessation is probably a sign of things to come. Better understanding of how smoking influences the brain will probably lead to better drugs to help smokers quit. So don't worry.

Try your best now. But also recognize that your efforts to quit are going to receive more types of assistance in the future.

Buproprion also illustrates the fact that quitting smoking requires attention to both the biology and psychology of smoking. Buproprion is helpful when used with education programs and support from health professionals or with an intensive self-help program.

As with all these help tools to quitting, there is still no magic cure. Buproprion will help smokers quit, but they have to take the first step and continue to work to keep temptations from undermining their efforts.

Alternative Medicine

If patches, pills and sprays don't appeal to you, then you might be interested in techniques that are often categorized as alternative medicine.

Two alternative therapies – hypnosis and acupuncture – have sparked particular interest as aids to quitting smoking.

Hypnosis is a state of attentive and focused concentration that is induced by the use of "therapeutic suggestion." The hypnotic trance state resembled other forms of deep relaxation. People cannot be hypnotized involuntarily and they do not follow hypnotic suggestions that are against their wishes. People who want to be helped are the best hypnotic subjects.

When employed by psychologists, physicians, and others trained in its use, hypnosis may help in quitting smoking.

Ask your doctor for a referral, or contact your local or state psychological association for the names of licensed psychologists in your area who practice hypnosis.

Like other therapies, though, it's not a magic solution that can be used alone. Hypnosis cannot make you quit or automatically eliminate all your desires to smoke. It should be part of a systematic quit smoking program.

Acupuncture is an ancient Chinese therapy that involves stimulating specific anatomic points in the body. This regulates or corrects the flow of "chi" (or energy) in the body, and thus restores health.

Puncturing the skin with a needle is the most typical method of acupuncture. As with all other therapies, acupuncture works best for smoking cessation when it's used in combination with a serious effort to quit and a behavior modification strategy to support their effort.

Questions to Ask Your Doctor

Before you start your countdown to quit day, do consider making an appointment with your doctor to discuss your plans. It doesn't matter if the doctor hasn't discussed smoking with you before.

Once approached, most doctors will be eager to help you plan a quit program that suits your personal and medical needs.

Your doctor may want to take baseline measurements of your heart rate, blood pressure, and weight. In addition, your doctor will determine whether you have any pre-existing medical conditions, such as impaired lung function or chest pains, which might show measurable improvement when you stop smoking.

This baseline information will be recorded in your medical chart. That way, you'll have a point of comparison when you return for follow-up visits after you've successfully quit.

Don't forget your dentist either. Tobacco use has a dramatic effect on the mouth, teeth, and gums. That's why most dentists are eager to help their patients quit smoking.

One good way to begin your quit program is to have your dentist clean your teeth, so you'll see some immediate improvement in your appearance right at the start.

Set Your Quit Day

You have come along way, and you've already made a lot of decisions. You have decided whether or not to try nicotine fading or one of the nicotine replacement therapies. Maybe you've decided to see your doctor to investigate the non-nicotine pill, or alternative therapies such as hypnosis or acupuncture.

Whatever you've decided so far, you have one more big decision to make. Now is the time to set a date to quit!

Pick a day to quit – about 7 to 14 days from now. Try to choose a day that makes personal sense to you. It should be one that fits your smoking patterns. But it should also reflect the other big things in your life (your family, your work, and how you like to relax and enjoy yourself). For example, many people choose a Monday, so they can start the week off right. Others quit on a Saturday morning so they have two days to get it down before having to spend a day in the office without cigarettes.

If you smoke a lot at work, you may want to quit over a weekend or maybe over a three-day weekend or holiday, if there is one coming up. If you are a relaxation smoker (and you smoke only on weekends or when you're home), you might want to quit on a Monday, so you have the whole workweek to get used to it before getting through a Friday or Saturday night without cigarettes.

Make your Quit Day something you feel personally committed to. But whatever day you choose, be sure to:

• Mark the date on your calendar. Circle it in red.
• Be determined to quit on that date.
• Spend plenty of time getting used to the idea.
• Cross off each day on the calendar as you count down to Quit Day.

Tell yourself that on that day, you will absolutely stop smoking. No fooling around, no kidding yourself, no halfway measures. Just quit. No more cigarettes!

Don't quit before your Quit Day. You need to work toward it and get ready for it. You're likely to look forward to your Quit Day and may want to quit a day or two earlier. But don't. Set your Quite Date and work toward it. Then quit.

# PREPARE FOR YOUR QUIT DAY

During the day, you have a lot of triggers that push you to smoke. And these triggers are responsible for most of your really strong urges to smoke. Ask yourself: "What's the cigarette that is toughest for me to go without?" Chances are your answer will be something like:

• The cigarette with the first cup of coffee in the morning.
• The cigarette right after a long movie.
• The relaxing cigarette after dinner.
• The cigarette at morning break, after not having one since you came to work.
• The cigarette with a drink you need to unwind when you get home in the evening.

Each of these descriptions centers on a trigger – the first cup of coffee, getting out of the movie, relaxing after dinner, morning break, and a drink in the evening. These triggers that you and your brain have come to associate with smoking – when they happen, you have to smoke. As a matter of fact, this association is so strong that you actually crave a cigarette as these triggers come up.

But there is a way to eliminate these tough "trigger" situations. If you can get rid of the cues for smoking before you quit, situations in which you've "just got to have a cigarette" will lose some of their power. And you can do it before you quit.

So let's start destroying these triggers. The first step is to identify your strongest triggers, the situations in which you always smoke. For example:

• Do you always smoke after dinner? With your morning coffee?
• Do you always light a cigarette when the phone rings?

When your children go off to school or get back home?
• Do you always smoke while driving in rush-hour traffic?
While driving from errand to errand?

These "always" situations are your strongest external triggers for smoking. First you'll have to eliminate these. Once you feel you feel less need to smoke at the very times you thought you could "never get through without a cigarette," then you'll feel less need in other, less strongly cued situations. Start eliminating these "always" triggers a week or two before your Quit Day.

The Key To Destroy Triggers

To destroy a trigger, you have to make the decision: "I will never smoke" when that trigger kicks in. For example, if you always smoke when you drink coffee, you must change your pattern so you never ever smoke while drinking coffee. This will definitely be hard at first, but it will keep to the "I will never" rule – and soon coffee will no longer be a cigarette trigger for you. This is how you can do it:

1) You will notice that you smoke during certain times and during certain situations. Make a list of when you light up and during which situation. (For example, after dinner). Smoking at these times has been so automatic for you that you don't even notice it.

2) Choose two or three times during which you smoke from your list. Be specific: "In the morning" is too broad. But "sitting in the car while driving to work," or "during afternoon break at work" are good.

3) Next make the commitment: I will never smoke when these specific triggers kick in. You will still drive to work, but think about doing something else while you drive. If you always listen to the radio as you drive and smoke.

Do not turn on the radio. That too is part of your trigger to smoke. And if you don't listen to the radio as you drive and smoke, then you should listen to the radio in order to break out of the mold in which you always smoke.

4) Once you choose triggers to destroy – DO NOT EVER SMOKE in these specific situations.

If this seems really hard, try to replace "won't" with "can't." For example, if your doctor told you that milk is life-threatening for you, you would probably find lots of ways to make sure you avoid milk. Think and act in the same way with cigarette. FIND WAYS TO AVOID THEM.

The way the powerful triggers have become so strongly linked to smoking is because they occur over and over when you smoke. If you've smoked a pack a day for 20 odd years, and drunk coffee with thousands of these cigarettes, that's a lot of time for the association to be firmly embedded in your mind.

Your body and your mind have learned that when coffee arrives, a cigarette isn't far. So when you drink coffee and there's no nicotine, you feel a huge urge to light up.

You can eliminate these triggers by starting not to smoke when you drink coffee. Just as you learned that coffee and cigarettes go hand-in-hand, you can also learn that they don't.

By using the "I will never" rule, you can get yourself used to coffee without cigarettes. And what's really fortunate is that you can do this in just the week or so before your Quit Day. Then, when you quit, the urges will be less strong.

For this destruction of triggers to work, you must totally separate the trigger from the cigarette. If coffee is a trigger, it won't work to drink a cup of coffee, and then have a cigarette, and then drink a second cup.

You must wait about 10-15 minutes after finishing your coffee before you light a cigarette. And then, don't follow up with another cup of coffee.

If talking on the telephone is your trigger – you must never light up while talking on the phone. If you're already smoking when the phone rings, you must either put out the cigarette – or just not answer the phone. Remember, the goal is to keep the trigger totally separate from smoking. Here are some quick tips to help you along:

1) Be consistent. It's better to choose two or three important triggers that you will never smoke with, instead of trying not to smoke with many different cues.

2) Don't try to quit smoking or even cut down yet. Gradually cutting down leads to stronger urges than quitting cold turkey. So keep smoking for now, but just decide NEVER to smoke in connection with the triggers you have chosen. You can still smoke at other times.

Some triggers for smoking are external (a cup of coffee, a ringing telephone, a waiting room). But some triggers are internal – the thoughts and feelings inside you that trigger your smoking. For example, you may reach for a cigarette when you feel angry, when you're feeling unsure of yourself.

Sometimes external triggers for smoking are a lot easier to recognize than internal triggers. As you stop smoking in response to external triggers, you'll probably become more aware of your internal triggers – the feelings and frustrations linked to your smoking.

For example, if you stop smoking during a business lunch where you usually would smoke, you'll probably notice feelings such as frustration or boredom that previously had been counteracted by your cigarette smoking.

This can help you understand why you always smoked during business lunches.

Keep track of the feelings and frustrations that are triggers for your smoking habit. Knowing which feelings really hit your cigarette button will help you spot the ones to work on.

For example, if sadness is a big trigger for you, make a point of saying, "I will never smoke when I am feeling sad." Then, by the time you get to your Quit Date, feeling sad will not be such a strong cue for smoking. You may still feel sad, but at least it will no longer be a trigger to smoke.

Eliminating your strong triggers before you quit will mean fewer strong urges to smoke when your Quit Day comes around. This is the real plus of destroying triggers. Also, it boosts your confidence. Seeing that you can control your strongest triggers will help you get the confidence you need to actually quit smoking.

Gaining Self-Control

Even though you eliminate your strong triggers for smoking, you are still going to have temptations to slip up and smoke. As we all know, temptations are hard to resist. It is relatively easy not to smoke cigarettes that you haven't bought. But, it's hard not to smoke the cigarette your friend offers you at coffee break, after a hectic morning.

You may forget your goal to have a long life when you're in a situation that tempts you to smoke. Often you just can't resist the short-term pleasure, the desire to just have one.

It's not as hopeless as it sounds. The important things to self-control are:

1) To anticipate temptations.

2) To use creative problem solving to keep the temptation from getting too close and to keep yourself from being able to yield to its temporary allure.

3) To do things – follow through with the strategies you created. Use them.

Remember, creativity ahead of time can be your weapon against temptation. And any strategy that blocks momentary temptations, or that keeps you from giving in to the temporary urge will increase your self-confidence and help you get to the long-term goal of enjoying life without cigarettes.

Anticipating Temptations

Think about the situations you are likely to be tempted in. There are a number of ways to approach them. Look at the moods you indicated: anxiety, sadness, or happiness. Times when you are especially anxious or feeling blue are likely to be especially tempting.

There may also be situations which don't occur too often, but when they do, it's hard to fight. Make a list of possible temptations that you are prone to.

After specifying your temptations, you need to think of specific things you will do to keep each from getting to you.

Here are some questions to ask to help you come up with good strategies:

• How can I avoid the temptation altogether?
• If I can't avoid it, how can I weaken the temptation when I feel tempted?
• What can I do ahead of time to reduce my urge when tempted?
• When tempted, how can I limit my ability to give in to the temptation?

Be creative, and get really specific in answering these questions. Now is not the time to be vague. Specific answers will be your best defense against temptation.

Here are some ideas that will help you get creative:

1) Change your environment. Get rid of all cigarettes, ashtrays, lighters, and matches.

2) Prepare yourself. Have creative alternatives available, such as sugar-free gum, low-calorie snacks, etc. Plan an enjoyable activity and start it before the temptation occurs (for example, take a walk after dinner).

3) Make use of your social world. Tell a lot of people that you've quit smoking. Make clear to your smoking friends that you don't want them to give you a cigarette (most relapse cigarettes come from friends). Tell a friend about an upcoming temptation and ask them to give you some encouragement in the situation (perhaps before a tense meeting).

4) Keep your goal in mind. Rehearse your reasons for quitting. Promise yourself something you enjoy (movie, dinner) for getting through the first week. Get involved in activities that don't go with smoking (exercise, meditation). Imagine yourself as you'd like to feel, enjoying favorite activities without smoking.

5) Reduce the appeal of temptations. Think about the harmful things cigarettes do to you. Think about the diseases you're concerned about if you go back to smoking. As you can see from these examples, your will-power does not depend on some inner strength – but it rests on how well you anticipate temptations and how creatively you act to change them.

Avoiding temptations is certainly a lot of work, and it requires effort in advance. But keep in mind the fact that quitting smoking is the most important, and one of the hardest things you'll do all year. Give it the attention that it (and you) deserves.

Cooperation and Encouragement

You're the one who puts a cigarette in your mouth and smokes it, but others can still play an important role in your smoking habit – and in your efforts to quit. Quitting goes a lot more smoothly and is more successful if you have cooperation and encouragement from your family and friends. Can you think of three people you can use for your quit team? Try to choose:

• One person from your immediate family.
• One person from work.
• One person from your circle of friends.

A spouse or family member can be a help when you quit. They will care a lot whether you quit and be willing to cooperate in ways that can really help.

Some people may hesitate to help you simply because they're not sure what they can do. It's up to you to tell them. If you want them to call you, tell them. If you don't want calls, let them know that too.

Here are some other ways that people can help you:

• Hear you out when you're tempted to smoke.
• Suggest methods for getting past the urge.
• Stop by to see you (or call you) on days you know will be hard for you.
• Help explain your needs to your spouse.
• Be available just to listen to you complain about how awful it is (or brag about how well you're doing).

Another way to let people know how you would like their encouragement or cooperation is to talk with them about it. Ask them to spend a few minutes with you on this. Here are some pointers to help you along:

For You the Quitter:

1. What does it mean to you for someone to be there?

2. When will you need people to put up with you – when you're crabby or cranky the first few days after you stop smoking? Or in the weeks following, when it is no longer a novelty.

3. How would you like others to cooperate with your efforts? Are there specific times you'll need them to give you some help?

4. Do you want to be asked how things are going or how you're doing? About how often or when?

5. Are there some prizes or rewards that you would like when you're been successful? Are there some that would be fun for both you and your family member or friend?

For the Friend or Family Member:

1. Be positive. Tell them how glad you are they've stopped smoking.

2. Reward and praise them. Rewards don't have to cost much, just use your imagination.

3. Don't nag. Focus on how hard they are trying and how much you recognize that.

4. Understand that they may want to talk about wanting a cigarette or having a relapse. This does not mean that they don't really want to quit.

5. Don't tell them how to feel. Accept and try to understand how they are feeling.

6. Don't tell them what to do. Ask them what they are thinking of doing and try to get them to think about the pros and cons.

7. If they slip up, encourage them not to give up.

In fact, it's a good idea to discuss these issues with other people too – your spouse, friends, and coworkers. Explain to them that you'd like them to be willing to listen when you ask for their time. If you'd rather that they let you bring up the subject first, tell them.

Working Together

If you're quitting with a friend or just lining up some encouragement for your own efforts, be sure to have phone numbers handy.

A telephone call can give you or your friend just the needed boost to help lift your mood and keep you from smoking. You and your friend may want to call each other, or get together, at a certain time each day.

Remember, quitting smoking is important, so think about scheduling specific times to meet or talk on the phone, just as you would a business appointment.

When people quit smoking they sometimes feel low, sorry for themselves, lonely, and deprived. That's when the encouragement of family or friends can be especially helpful. If you think you are going to be feeling sorry for yourself for a few days, tell others ahead of time and discuss what you can plan to combat it.

Often people will feel they don't know what to say. Some well-intentioned things people say may be misinterpreted as "nagging" or "bossy." So tell your friends anything you think is important to know about you and what kind of "helpful suggestions" you can deal with.

Planning Alternatives to Smoking

The key to quitting is to plan ahead. So far, you've made plans for dealing with temptations and you've planned to recruit support people. Now you've got to plan specific activities that can take the place of smoking.

You'll definitely need things to do with your hands and mouth. Some people suck on stirring sticks, or fiddle with paper clips. Others go for a brisk walk. Many people find that a few deep breaths work best. Calling up one of your support people can also help. Or sit down and write a letter, or read a book.

Chewing gum can help. If you're using nicotine gum, be sure to have several pieces with you at all times.

These activities may not discourage urges but at least they'll give you something to do instead of just sitting there, craving that cigarette.

Here's something to do before you stop smoking. Pack a survival kit of things you can use to keep your hands and mouth busy whenever you're tempted to smoke. Keep your survival kit with you at all times.

You can put the following items in your survival kit:

• Stirring sticks
• Sugarless gum
• Sugarless candy
• A ball to squeeze
• Cinnamon sticks
• Rubber bands
• Paper clips
• A pencil to hold

Keeping busy is also important to keep your mind off smoking. Plan ahead to get together often with friends, schedule outdoor activities, and stock up on magazines and videos. If you don't have a hobby, this is good time to start one. You may also need to spend more time with people who don't smoke. So try going places where smoking is not allowed.

Diet and Exercise

You can, of course, eat and drink as an alternate to smoking. Food and drink can indeed be a convenient and tempting substitute. Also, you may find yourself hungry more often after you give up smoking. Quitting also can cause metabolic changes that lead to an initial weight gain.

So be prepared. Here are some hints to help you:

• Keep a supply of healthy snacks like fruits or veggie sticks on hand.
• Drink a large glass of water or a low-calorie beverage whenever you feel the urge to smoke.
• Instead of eating and drinking, try exercising (even just for a walk around the block) to keep your mind off smoking.

And remember, just because you're depriving yourself from cigarettes, it doesn't mean that you have to deprive yourself from your favorite food. You are likely concerned about weight gain, but you don't have to eliminate foods that you enjoy.

Eat a good, balanced diet. The best foods to include are:
• Fruits
• Vegetables
• Beans
• Whole grain bread
• Rice
• Pastas

If you fill up on these foods, you're less likely to be tempted by calories and pastries.

Exercise helps too. If you haven't exercised very much before, talk to your doctor about a sensible exercise program. There's no need to become a prime athlete overnight, but there are many good reasons to start a regular regimen of brisk walking, bicycle riding, swimming, or any other physical activity you enjoy.

Exercise will increase your metabolic rate and help your body burn extra calories. Exercise also helps reduce tension and stress, which will make you feel more relaxed and alert. Also these benefits can be a big help to you in quitting smoking and minimizing weight gain.

Focusing on diet and exercise is a healthy part of your quitting plan. But don't get so busy with these concerns that you lose sight of your real goal. Remember, your real goal is quitting smoking.

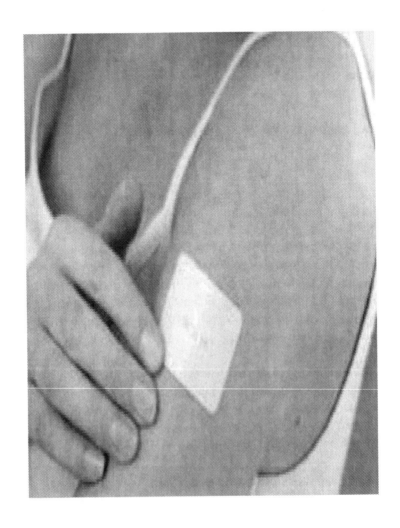

# TOOLS AND TIPS TO HELP YOU QUIT

There are many resources available to smokers nowadays to help them butt out. It is a good idea to find out what is out there for you to help in your efforts to quit smoking. Here is a list and description of some of them:

E-Z QUIT:

This is a plastic "cigarette" that contains a peppermint-menthol flavored capsule, which you can puff away on. There is no smoke, no ashes, no nicotine, and no damage to your health. You can use E-Z Quit while cutting down after quitting. Because there's no smoke, you can even puff away in no-smoking areas.

The plastic "cigarette" lasts indefinitely, although the mint flavor disappears after three to four weeks. A 90-day supply of capsules is included when you first buy E-Z Quit. Additional capsules are available. You can order E-Z Quit from:

The Center for Self-Care Studies
3805 Stevenson Avenue
Austin, TX 78703
(512) 458-9333

LIFESIGN QUIT-SMOKING COMPUTER:

This is a tiny computer (the size of a fat credit card), which is programmed to help you taper down gradually before quitting. Several weeks before your chosen quitting day, you press a button to activate the mechanism, then carry the LifeSign with you at all times. For the first week, you press the "smoke" button on the device each time you light a cigarette. Beginning on the first day of the second week, you smoke only when the computer tells you it's time for a cigarette.

81

The computer beeps each time a cigarette is allowed. It starts you at your normal smoking rate. The intervals between cigarettes get longer and longer over a period of two to four weeks immediately before your chosen quitting day. On your quit day and thereafter, the device flashes a "no smoking" symbol. For more information you can contact:

Health Innovations
13873 Park Center Road
Suite 336
Herndon, VA 22071
(800) 543-3744 or (703) 478-2824

LUNG CHECK:

This is a home sputum test designed to serve as an early warning system for smokers by identifying tissue damage at a time when quitting smoking can still reverse the progression of the disease. In addition to screening for lung cancer, the test looks for signs of six other biological responses to cigarette smoke.

The Lung Check is designed to be repeated at regular intervals. Test results are given in a graphic format that allows the smoker to evaluate positive or negative trends in lung function. The test can thus be used by smokers to determine the extent of existing damage or by recent quitters to document improvement in lung function.

The Lung Check is normally marketed directly to physicians. But the company will also provide the test directly to interested individuals. Those who order the test will receive a stamped, mail-in sputum container, a brochure on smoking and your lungs, and instructions for collecting a sputum sample. The user collects three morning sputum samples and mails them back to the lab.

The results arrive by mail. You have to include the name and phone number of your primary physician with your order. The lab will phone your physician if the results suggest that further testing is needed. Call or write:

CytoSciences
Lung Check Division
1601 Saratoga Sunnyvale Road
Cupertino, CA 95014
(800) 433-8278 or (408-996-0600

## HEALTH BANK:

This method provides financial rewards for positive steps toward quitting. As part of your commitment to quit, you pledge to put aside a certain amount of money each week. This money can be kept in a special envelope or bank account. You receive the money when you have gone without smoking for 100 days (or any length of time you prefer). You can even ask some of your support people to contribute to your health bank.

## THE RUBBER BAND METHOD:

This method is actually backed by research. You wear a rubber band around your wrist and snap it against your skin when you feel the urge to smoke. Be sure that the rubber band is loose enough so it doesn't block blood flow or leave a mark on the skin when it is removed.

## CLONIDINE:

A recent study suggests that the drug Clonidine (marketed under the brand name Catapres) significantly reduces withdrawal symptoms and nicotine cravings among recent quitters. Clonidine is often prescribed for high blood pressure. The drug seems to reduce cigarette cravings significantly. This does not mean that the drug is a cure for smoking, since some people will continue to smoke despite taking clonidine. The side effects of this drug are dizziness and drowsiness. If you are receiving Medical treatment for hypertension, ask your doctor if it would be appropriate for you to switch to clonidine. Some physicians may be willing to prescribe clonidine for a prospective quitter even if they do not have Hypertension (particularly those with serious smoking-related illnesses, such as emphysema).

STOP-SMOKING GROUPS:
You can contact the following groups that have excellent support programs for people who wish to quit:

Action on Smoking and Health (ASH)
2013 H. Street, NW
Washington, DC 20006
(202) 659-4310

American Lung Association
1740 Broadway
New York, NY 10019
(212) 315-8700

American Cancer Society
4 West 35th Street
New York, NY 10001
(212) 736-3030

The Breathe-Free Plan for Stop Smoking
Narcotics Education Inc.
6830 Laurel Street, NW
Washington, DC 20012

Smokers Anonymous
PO Box 25335
West Los Angeles, CA 90025
(212) 474-8997

Aside from the above resources, there are also various tips that you can use to help you in your efforts at quitting.

Here are some of these tips:

1) Keep your hands busy. Knit a sweater. Write letters. Do crosswords. Read a book. Make puzzles. Take up drawing or painting.

2) Take frequent showers. Whenever you feel like smoking, take a long hot shower instead.

3) Clove oil. Anytime you get the urge to smoke, put a drop of clove oil on your finger and apply it to the back of your tongue. You buy clove oil at most health food stores.

4) Licorice sticks. This is not the candy, but the actual licorice twigs, which you can buy at natural food stores. They have a pleasant taste and give you mouth and hands something to do.

5) Sunflower seeds. Buy a few pounds of sunflower seeds, and whenever you feel the urge to smoke, take out a handful and eat these instead. As you crack the shell and take out the kernels, you will keep your hands really busy.

6) Brush your teeth right after meals. Often the urge to smoke is really intense right after meals. So it is a good idea to get up from the table right after you eat, head into the bath, and brush and floss your teeth.

7) Cut down on alcohol, because all too often a cigarette and a drink are very closely linked.

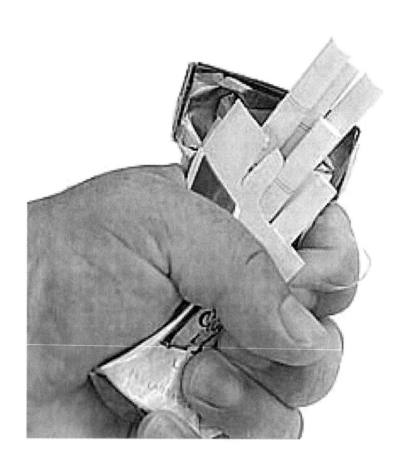

# QUITTING

Your Quit Day is one of the most important days of your life. You have gotten ready to quit. You have thought about it. You understand your smoking habit and you know why you want to quit. You've learned many things to help you make it over the next few weeks without smoking.

You can do it! You're well prepared and ready to be smoke-free for life. Soon you will be the nonsmoker you want to be.

## The Day Before

It is important to quit with determination, not with a whimper. Stay focused, and get your energy and confidence concentrated on the big change you're making in your life.

Quitting is a big step, a major change in your life. It's natural to be worried and nervous. Try to think of yourself as being more geared up and excited than worried and nervous. Think about why you want to do this. Make sure you are clear on your reasons for quitting.

To make you feel more confident, review your plans now and you'll realize you really have arranged to make this a success. Ask yourself: How have you done in eliminating the cigarettes associated with your strongest urges? If you've done well, your quitting will be a lot easier because those killer cigarettes won't be half as big an issue as you had feared. Here are important questions to think about:

• What creative alternatives do you have lined up to take the place of cigarettes?
• What are your will-power strategies for fighting temptation after you quit?

• What plans do you have for getting cooperation and encouragement from your family and friends?

When you review these questions, you will gain confidence, because you will feel prepared. It will be hard because you will be giving up something that you will really miss. But stay determined and be well prepared.

Here are some points to keep in mind as you begin to get ready for the big day:

1) Quitting smoking is important and difficult. You are taking on a big task. So remember to be nice to yourself. Cut yourself some slack. If you can become smoke-free in the next few weeks, you don't need to do anything else to prove you're a hero.

2) Plan an easy day for your Quit Day. You may want it to be a busy one, so you have lots of distractions. Or you may want it to be a relaxing one. Regardless, try to make it a day with the fewest demands possible.

3) Remind your family and friends that you're counting on their cooperation and encouragement in the next week or two. You might want to ask someone you think is really understanding to spend some time hearing you out about your feelings.

4) Make sure you reward yourself. If you haven't planned some reward for the first day or two, you should consider it. Rewards are not the reason you quit, but they can help show to yourself that what you're doing is important and that it's worth a little enjoyment. Of course, the best reward is quitting itself. But you deserve many more rewards for not smoking. Rewards don't have to be big and expensive (they can even be free). But reward yourself with things you care about or like.

## Start Spreading the News

Before you quit it is a good idea to tell your friends, your family, and your coworkers that you are going to be smoke-free as of tomorrow. Even those whom you are not going to look to for support should still know.

The more people around you who know you are quitting, the less you will want to give in to temptations. Also, many people will want to help you quit and will be happy to give you some encouragement.

Quitting is an important step for you, but there are sure to be some unhappy people who won't understand what you're going through and may not make it easy for you. But don't let anyone put you down. Rehearse in your mind how you'll reply to negative comments.

## Nicotine Replacement

If you're planning to use nicotine gum, nicotine patches, or any other form of nicotine replacement, be sure you have these items on hand, so they'll be ready for use. Do read the instructions thoroughly, but don't start using any of these products until you eventually stop smoking.

You must quit smoking completely before you use any nicotine replacement. If you don't follow this important caution, you could develop serious side effects caused by an overdose of nicotine.

If your doctor has prescribed Zyban (the non-nicotine pill) or any other medications, be sure that you are taking this medication as directed, so that it will be an effective level in your body on your Quit Day.

Your Creative Alternatives

In preparation for your Quit Day, today is also a good day to get out your Survival Kit that you packed. Be sure you have a good supply of sugarless candy and gum, drink-stirring sticks, and any other items you can turn to when you feel tempted by cigarettes.

Spend some time thinking about when you will use the creative alternatives you have identified for yourself. You might even pick a couple of situations during the day when you would normally have a cigarette, such as while talking on the phone or after dinner. Instead, try one of your creative alternatives.

Learn to Relax and Relieve Stress

Simply reviewing all your preparations and thinking about the challenge ahead will make most people a bit tense and nervous. This is the time to exercise and relieve stress, or do a bit of relaxation exercisers Here's what you can do:

• Sit down anywhere and close your eyes.
• Think about something that makes you feel good.
• Relax your shoulders. Close your mouth. Inhale slowly and as deeply as you can. Keep your shoulders relaxed.
• Hold your breath while you count to four.
• Exhale slowly, letting out all of the air from your lungs.
• Slowly repeat these steps five times.

Do these relaxing exercises at least once every day at least until you feel secure that you are done with cigarettes. You may want to do it more often in the next couple of weeks. It is a great creative alternative to smoking.

The Night Before Your Quit Day

• Be good to yourself. Eat food you like. Watch a video.
Take a long bath.
• Get a good night's sleep and be well rested for the big day
ahead. (Tonight you'll have your last cigarette).
• Get rid of all the cigarettes in the house.
• Look for any cigarettes that may be in the pockets of your
clothes in the cupboards, in your office, in your car. Get rid
of all of them now. Run water on them or crumble them up,
if that helps.

• Get rid of ashtrays, lighters, and matches.
• Go through your reasons for not smoking. Reflect on what
they mean to you. Try to add another reason to your list.
• Try to go to sleep feeling good about yourself. You are
about to do something that will be hard, but will give you
lots of satisfaction for many years to come.

Your Quit Day

This is the big day! You're well prepared and ready to be
smoke-free. You've waited for it, dreaded it at times, and
maybe even looked forward to it. Feel confident as you take
the big step in this very important accomplishment.

To get your day started right, get up right away and head
straight for the shower. If you've been accustomed to
smoking immediately on waking up, this quick shower will
help you start right on your first day as a nonsmoker.

If you're going to use nicotine gum or the nicotine patch,
now is the time to start. Follow the directions on the
package or in the guidelines given to you by your doctor.

Get dressed and eat breakfast pretty quickly this morning.
If your usual routine is to linger over breakfast coffee with a
cigarette, skip coffee today. Or buy it on your way to work
– in a shop where no smoking is allowed.

When eating lunch, taking a work break, or going out to shop, choose places where smoking is not allowed. And for your first few days as a nonsmoker try to make an effort to spend more time with people who don't smoke. On the other hand, if you are going to be with smokers, tell people ahead of time that you have quit and that they should not offer you a cigarette.

If you're with people whom you don't know well, you may feel somewhat uncomfortable with this announcement. But many people will congratulate you. If someone does slip and offers you a cigarette, remember to say a firm "No!" to temptation.

Today also may be a good time to keep your schedule pretty full, so you won't have time on your hands. Line up some easy chores, favorite magazines, or jobs that must get done right away, that way, if you have even a few minutes with nothing to do, you can immediately keep yourself busy.

Think about all the difficult things you try to do in life: eating well, staying organized, and keeping the pile of bills on your desk to a minimum. In a lot of way, quitting smoking is harder than each of these. But here's a good way of looking at it: Once you put out that last cigarette, you became an ex-smoker. You don't have to do anything more.

In contrast, think about someone who needs to lose twenty pounds. They can work hard for a week, lose three pounds, feel great for a moment, and then they realize they still have to lose about 15 more! Or think about yourself and exercising, doing the laundry, or paying the bills. You feel great that you got a good workout today, got fresh sheets on all the beds, or got the desk clear. But tomorrow and next week and next month, you'll need to exercise, do the laundry, or pay the bills all over again.

Of course, staying off cigarettes is going to be hard, especially over the next week or so. But if you can stay off, you've reached your goal. You don't have to do anything more and you don't have to quit again tomorrow or next week or next month.

The first day of quitting is tough. You may feel you have little energy to do much else than hold on. It's normal to have a hard time today. It doesn't really mean there's anything wrong with you. And it certainly doesn't mean that your case is too hard, that you can't quit. So don't be scared. Be easy on yourself.

Symptoms of Recovery

Quitting smoking brings on a variety of physical and psychological symptoms. Of course, there is no way to avoid all the physical effects, but what can help is knowing what to expect, and how to deal with it.

For some people, coping with recovery symptoms is like riding a roller coaster. Most symptoms decrease after the first few days. Some stop totally after about three days. But some may get worse after a day or two. This may be partly psychological – the first day or two, your enthusiasm may keep you from recognizing some of your reactions to quitting. But most symptoms pass within two to four weeks.

Here are some of the most common symptoms, and the best ways to relieve them.

Irritability. Use the method described above to relieve stress. Take walks, hot baths, and use nicotine replacement.

Fatigue. Take naps, try to take it easy, and be gentle on yourself. Try nicotine replacement.

Insomnia. Use the stress relief method. Avoid caffeine, including chocolate after 6PM.

Cough. Dry throat. Nasal drip. Drink plenty of fluids, and use cough drops.

Dizziness. Use extra caution driving, operating machinery, and climbing stairs. Change positions slowly.

Poor concentration. Plan workload accordingly. Avoid unnecessarily demanding assignments during the first week.

Constipation/Gas. Drink plenty of fluids, and add roughage to your diet (fruits, vegetables, whole grain cereals).

Hunger. Drink water or low-calorie liquids. Be prepared with low-calorie snacks.

Craving for a cigarette. Try one of your creative alternatives, and wait out the urge (urges only last a few minutes). Distract yourself, exercise, and go for a walk.

No matter how hard you plan, you're sure to hit a few situations where you're really dying for a cigarette. Don't start to panic.

Craving a cigarette is often the most difficult side effect of quitting. If you have trouble remembering all your creative alternatives, or if you're caught without a plan and have a really strong craving, here some quick tips to help you.

1. Delay. The urge to smoke will pass whether you smoke or not.

2. Deep breathing will help you relax and release stress.

3. Drink lots of water. This will help ease many of the symptoms of quitting.

4. Do something to take your mind off smoking.

Also, don't forget your alternative activities. Chew on a stirring stick. If you're using nicotine gum, remember to chew it frequently during the day. Make a telephone call. Take a walk. Even if you're inside at home or in an office, you can walk into another room, pick up something to read for a few minutes, or go to the bathroom and brush your teeth.

If you're still finding it hard to control your urge, call one of your key friends or family members. Follow through on your plan to contact them for encouragement. If you need their help, or even just to hear them lecture you, do it. It will help.

Of course, plans are easier to make than to keep. Most often people stop doing the things that will help them stay off cigarettes. They may get distracted by their own discomfort or by other activities in their lives or they may just "forget."

But stick to your plan. Make it a priority. Remember:

1) Quitting smoking is one of the most important things you'll do all year. It deserves your time and attention even if that means putting some other important things "on hold" for a little while.

2) Practice healthy selfishness. If you slip, you will be responsible. But it's your right today and for the next few weeks and months to do the things you need to do to stay off cigarettes.

## Immediate Benefits

Right now, while you're concentrating on getting through the day without smoking, it's probably difficult to focus on the benefits of quitting. But this can be a great tool for success. For many people, recognizing benefits is an excellent source of motivation to keep on resisting the urge.

Did you know that your body is already starting to show the benefits of quitting? In fact, the moment you quit smoking, your body began to repair the damage.

Within a half hour of your last cigarette, your blood pressure and pulse rate began to move back to normal.

Within merely eight hours, the carbon monoxide level in your blood dropped to normal and your oxygen level increased.

By quitting just for one day, you have already decreased your chance of having a sudden heart attack!

You're well on the road to a longer, healthier, happier life.

# THE FIRST TWO NON-SMOKING WEEKS

You've made it past your first day without smoking. You may not have thought you could do it – but you have!

Think a little about how you feel about this. Don't let your victory go unnoticed. Here are questions to think about:

• Why do you think you were successful?
• Where did you almost trip but kept going?
• How did you manage to avoid getting tripped up?
• How does this make you feel about your chances of staying off cigarettes?

As you answer these questions, you will begin to feel a little proud of yourself! Enjoy the feeling, and use it as a springboard to keep going.

You probably don't feel like a new person as yet but you are already changing. You're likely to feel more energetic and more alive than you have in years. A lot of self-repair work is already going on inside you. Your body is at work repairing smoke-damage tissues this very minute. You may not notice the changes yet, but you will.

## It's Tough

Reading about the wonderful advantages of quitting may not be so comforting to you if you're feeling symptoms of recovery. You feel very cranky. You may have discovered nerves you never knew you had. You may be ready to take someone's head off for the most stupid reason. And you desperately want to smoke and get back to feeling "normal" with a cigarette in your hands.

All these feelings are normal, even if you're having them all at once. It's no secret that quitting can be a very tough job.

Remember that you have accomplished things successfully when you're angry. You've accomplished things when you were nervous and you have accomplished things when you felt sick. Your physical and emotional feelings don't have to direct your actions. You can quit in spite of them!

The first week is usually the worst. After that, the cravings lessen and lessen. Each day you will feel better and better.

Remember, things will get better. Most of the symptoms don't last long – a week or two at the most. Of course, a week or two seems an awfully long time. But after your first week of not smoking, the nicotine finally will be out of your system, and much of the tension you feel, as well as some of the other physical symptoms, will disappear.

This isn't to say that you won't have cravings after the first week. You probably will. But they will become weaker and less frequent, and easier to deal with.

Right now, though, you're still in the learning stage. Quitting is an extended process, not a single act. You still need to learn to become a permanent non-smoker.

Breaking the Nicotine Addiction Cycle

The physical recovery may be the most difficult during the first week or two. When you were smoking, you felt nervous and tense when your body craved nicotine.

When you smoked a cigarette, you felt better because the craving was temporarily satisfied. But as the nicotine disappeared from your system, your nicotine craving again increased, and you again felt nervous and tense.

You're quit smoking now, but your body is still caught up in the nicotine addiction stress cycle.

You have withdrawn the addictive substance (nicotine) and that has caused a traumatic jolt to your whole body. The result for many people is a huge assortment of changes in your eating, sleeping, breathing, digestion, thinking, and everything else your body does.

What's important to remember is that while you were taking nicotine by smoking many times each day, your body was not functioning normally. It seemed normal to you. But in reality you were always "Under the Influence" of nicotine. Now that the nicotine is gone, your body is working to relearn what is normal.

Signs of Physical Recovery

Right now, you are probably all too familiar with some of the symptoms of nicotine withdrawal. Reading about them won't make them go away. But understanding them may make them a little easier to tolerate.

Most importantly, remember these are not new problems that have now become part of your life. They're just your body getting back to normal. Here are some of these problems.

Irritability. This is perhaps the most commonly reported reaction of people giving up cigarettes. In removing the effects of nicotine as well as hundreds of other chemicals found in smoke, you have caused your body considerable stress. It's understandable that you may feel short-fused for the first few days.

Knowing to expect this normal reaction may help to keep it under control. So be easy on yourself and don't expect to be perfect during this stressful period.

Nervousness. This is part of irritability. You might want to ask your family, friends, and coworkers to understand that this is only a temporary effect that will disappear. Drink lots of liquids, especially fruit juices, to flush the nicotine out of your system as fast as possible. And avoid or limit stimulants like caffeine in coffee and cola drinks. Try decaf.

Coughing. This symptom may increase too because your lungs are cleaning themselves out, getting rid of residues built up from years of smoking. Smoking deadens the cilia in the lungs. These are little hair-like cells that help brush out dust and other residues in normal, healthy lungs. One of the reasons smokers have more infections is that their cilia are not working, so foreign matter accumulates in their lungs. When you quit, the cilia get back to work within a couple of days.

The result is that you start coughing up more phlegm and sputum. Sometimes, smokers see this and get scared because they think that they have some new problem. But it's not a problem at all – just another example of your body getting back to normal. This "ex-smoker's cough" is temporary and usually lasts only a week or two at most.

Cough drops or cough syrups will relieve most of this cough in the meantime.

Slight sore throat. This is another common symptom. Although tobacco irritates your throat, it also numbs it. So when you stop smoking you may feel some brief discomfort as your throat returns to its natural, normal state. Water and fruit juices can help.

Constipation. This is another sign that your body is readjusting itself to the lack of nicotine. Drink plenty of water and supplement your diet with fiber from fruits and whole grains.

Sleeping problems. This is a result of tension. Use the stress release exercisers described on page 90 and other relaxation techniques like deep breathing and a long, hot bath. Take a long walk to work off your nervous tension. If you fall asleep normally but wake in the middle of the night, you may be missing the nicotine your brain was used to. Consider using a nicotine replacement product during the day to give your body some of the nicotine it's missing. If you still have trouble sleeping, talk to your health care provider.

Tiredness/Fatigue. This often occurs as your body readjusts to functioning without the artificial stimulation of nicotine, especially if you're having trouble sleeping. You may have headaches too. Try to increase your exercise or allow yourself a little extra time for sleeping.

Difficulty concentrating. Many smokers rely on nicotine for alertness. In a short time, you will find this gets better. Your intense focus on quitting may also cause your mind to block out other thoughts. Nicotine replacement therapy can help.

The Psychological Recovery Process

Many smokers are only slightly bothered by physical symptoms of nicotine withdrawal, but experience a lot more trouble with the psychological symptoms of recovery. Getting over the psychological loss can be very complex. It may even take several months for you to restructure a lifestyle without smoking.

The reaction to giving up smoking can be like the reaction to death. Something dear to you is gone forever. It was something dangerous, but it was something that you were used to and liked in many ways, maybe because it made you feel sophisticated or able to handle things or attractive or sexy. Maybe it relaxed you and put you in a better mood.

Think of giving up smoking like the death of a close friend. A cigarette has been your friend. It was always there for you. It didn't tell you that you were making a mistake or that you were being unreasonable. It never got angry with you or demanding. Instead, it made you feel more relaxed and confident about what you were doing.

Any time we experience a major change in our lives, we grieve for the old ways before we learn to make room for the new. Here is what you should be working on:

1) Reject the feeling that you have given something up. It's actually the opposite – because you have gained something – your freedom and self-mastery.

2) Quitting is not an exercise in self-denial, but in self-determination. You're now in charge of your life again. You have a tremendous sense of self-control.

3) You are giving a gift to yourself and to those near you.

4) You are getting rid of a harmful habit. You're working hard, and you're getting important benefits in return.

5) You deserve a lot of praise for your efforts. Give yourself a big pat on the back. Reward yourself in small and big ways.

Replacing the Psychological Benefits of Cigarettes

As you go through the stages of physical and psychological recovery, you will have lots of feelings. Chewing stirring sticks or going for walks might help control urges to smoke when you're bored or fidgety. But these creative alternatives won't do as long-term substitutes for the cigarettes you used to control your feelings.

Not smoking will be easier if you keep in touch with your feelings, likes, dislikes, worries, and irritations. Start taking your feelings into account. Instead of just saying to yourself, "I need a cigarette," ask yourself what feeling is leading you to this question. If you can get in touch with that feeling you can begin to find better ways than smoking to handle it.

When tempted to reach for a cigarette, ask yourself:

• What am I feeling?
• Why am I having this feeling?
• What do I really want now?

You will find that often what you want is not a cigarette, but something else.

Dealing With Bad Moods

Sometimes you feel sad, anxious, or frustrated for good reasons. Bad things do happen. But there are other times you may get down on yourself because you're judging yourself too harshly or negatively. If you're like most people, you sometimes blow things out of proportion or over-react to incidents you would generally find only mildly annoying. And, as much as it happens to all of us, blowing things out of proportion can be a big problem when you're quitting smoking.

Once you quit smoking, what else can you do? Here are a few practical alternatives:

1) Check your assumptions. When you're upset or in a bad mood, write down what you're thinking and feeling. Then question why you feel the way you do. Here are some assumptions you may be making about yourself. They may make you feel bad about yourself and may make you want to smoke:

• I should never disappoint anyone.
• I need to be loved or liked by everyone.
• I should be such a good and worthy person that everyone will treat me with respect.
• In order to be happy, I have to be successful in everything I do.
• If I make a mistake, it shows I'm not really very good.
• If someone disagrees with me they don't think much of me.
• My worth as a person depends on what other people think of me.
• Life is fair. If I am a nice person, if I'm cheerful, if I do my best for others, bad things won't happen to me. If bad things do happen to me, it means I just haven't been good enough.

2) Change your expectations. If you find yourself expecting to be perfect with your family, if you find yourself feeling you always need to be on time, if you find yourself upset whenever anyone shows they're less than delighted with you (whatever may be the mistakes you're making in judging yourself), try to figure out a more realistic way of looking at things.

The Reward Cigarette

Stress and bad feelings can lead to cravings. But many people also smoke when they feel good. If you're one of them, you may often think, "I deserve this cigarette." After you've quit smoking, you won't be able to reward yourself with a cigarette. So you'll have to work on new rewards. For example:

• Ask yourself what healthy activity would make you feel good right now, and would make you feel rewarded.
• Make a list of nonsmoking activities to do to make yourself feel good (call a friend, see a movie, visit some place, etc.).

Positive Self-Talk

Tell yourself good things about yourself. This is a good way to combat bad moods. Many people spend too much time telling themselves they can't do things, aren't doing a good job, aren't capable. That's all negative self-talk. On the other hand, positive self-talk simply reverses all that by changing the negative thoughts into "I can do it" statements. For example:

• I can do it if I take it one day at a time. It will get easier with time if I just persist.
• I can get the same relaxed feeling if I sit and chat with a cup of tea and a good book.
• I feel good when I do what's really good for me. This decision to quit smoking is important to me.

Here are positive self-statements that you can use to help you think more rationally and calmly:

• I should think about what I really want for myself.
• Relax. I can calm down with a slow, deep breath.
• I can handle this. Take one step at a time.
• This is a chance for me to use what I have learned.
• Tough times don't last.
• Look for solutions.
• Stop. Look on the positive side.
• I can get support, advice, and help if I need it.

And here are some specific smoking-related, positive self-statements:

• Cigarettes make me cough, feel breathless, trigger heart trouble, and cause lung cancer.
• Cigarettes deprive me of life and health.
• Quitting has shown me personal strengths I didn't know I had.

Managing Stress

Physical craving for nicotine causes stress, along with the psychological stress of quitting.

When you were a smoker, you usually had cigarettes to reduce your stress. Now you seem to have no skills for dealing with stressful situations.

You need both short-term and long-term solutions to stress. The short-term help will get you through the day. The long-term solution is to figure out what's causing the stress and try to change it. Exercise is a great way to combat stress. Here are some other useful suggestions:

1) Get up 15 minutes earlier in the morning. The inevitable morning mishaps will be less stressful.

2) Prepare for the morning, the evening before. Set the breakfast table. Make lunches. Put out the clothes you plan to wear.

3) Don't rely on your memory. Write down appointment times, when to pick up the laundry, when library books are due, etc.

4) Make copies of all keys. Bury a house key in a secret spot in the garden. Carry a duplicate car key in your wallet.

5) Practice preventive maintenance. Your car, appliances, home and relationships will be less likely to break down at the worst possible moment.

6) Be prepared to wait. A paperback book can make a wait in line almost pleasant.

7) Procrastination is stressful. Whatever you want to do tomorrow, do today. Whatever you want to do today, do it now.

8) Plan ahead. Don't let the gas tank get below one-quarter full. Keep a well-stocked "emergency shelf" of home supplies. Don't wait until you're down to your last bus token or postage stamp to buy more.

9) Don't put up with something that doesn't work right. If your alarm clock, wallet, or shoelaces are a constant aggravation, fix them or get new ones.

10) Allow 15 minutes extra time to get to appointments. Plant to arrive at airport one hour before your flight.

11) Eliminate (or restrict) the caffeine in your diet.

12) Relax your standards. This world will not end if something does not get done.

13) Say no to extra projects, social activities, and invitations you know you don't have the time or energy for. Unplug your phone when you want to take a long bath, meditate, sleep, or read without interruption.

Deep Breathing Techniques

This exercise will show you how to breathe without cigarettes in a way that slows down the pace of your whole body and therefore promotes general relaxation. Deep breathing should be done using your stomach muscles as well as your lungs.

Before doing this exercise, put a hand on your abdomen. As you inhale deeply, feel your stomach pull in toward your spine. When you exhale, feel your stomach muscles release.

As you do the exercise, pause comfortably at the end of each exhalation until you feel ready to take the next deep breath.

Think of your lungs as balloons that you are trying to fill as completely as possible.

Here is the exercise:

1) Breathe in deeply, letting your stomach expand until your lungs are filled. Pause for a moment and then exhale until your lungs are emptied.

2) Pause for a moment, and then take another deep breath, filling your lungs completely.

3) Hold for a moment, and now let the airflow out, focusing your mind on restful thoughts.

4) Keeping the pace regular, again breathe in deeply, hold a moment, and now let the air out, feeling more and more relaxed.

5) Take another breath in, hold it for a moment, and gently breathe out, and let the tension escape from your body.

6) Once more, breathe in, pause a moment, now exhale, and feel the deep relaxation.

After you've learned how to do it, you can achieve even greater relaxation if you close your eyes during deep breathing. Let you mind focus on a restful scene or a word like "calm" to give you a feeling of mental quiet.

Your Will-Power Plans

Now that you are a nonsmoker, you need to actively review your plans for coping with temptations. Look back at the temptations you identified and the plans you had for coping with them. Which ones have you tried so far? Which ones have worked and which ones have not worked as well as you expected?

Based on your results so far, you want to revise your list. Concentrate on things that helped you stay off cigarettes.

Now think of two or three situations coming up this week that may make you want to smoke. Then think of two or three things you could do instead of smoking.

You may also want to treat moods and feelings like temptations, and work out a plan for coping with these emotions that will make you want to smoke. If an important meeting next Monday is making you anxious, make sure that you do some "defense tactics" to make sure you don't resort to smoking to deal with stress. For example:

• Take extra care to allow ample time for the task, so meeting your deadline won't be stressful.
• Plan fifteen-minute walks both morning and afternoon over the weekend to keep things a little calmer.
• Ask your spouse to give you encouragement over the weekend. Be sure to say exactly how you want to be encouraged (a pep talk, a hug, etc.).
• Plan your work so you can take a 10 minute break every hour to do your breathing exercise.
• Make sure you plan some things you'll enjoy doing over the weekend so the anxiety of making the deadline won't be compounded by feeling sad that you don't have enough fun.
• Make sure the area where you work does not have any reminders of smoking so you are not caught off guard.

You have to identify the right strategy for you. Find out what your temptations are, and then come up with specific strategies that you feel good about.

One word of advice, don't take a drink to relax – because drinking alcohol will increase your urge to smoke.

Remember, quitting smoking is a long process. You have to work on your will power first and foremost. People lapse when they let temptation come over them without doing anything about it. It doesn't matter so much what you do as long as it makes sense for you. But you do need to do something to keep those temptations at bay.

What If Will Power Does Not Work?

Of course, nobody's perfect. There will be times when all your creative alternatives and will power will not work against a tough temptation. When things don't go well, ask yourself:

• Could I have anticipated the temptation sooner?
• Did I look at all aspects of the temptation situation that I could change or avoid?
• Did I make a concrete plan?
• Did I carry out my plan or just think about it?

Different control strategies work for different people. Don't give up if a strategy that works for other people fails for you.

Try something else. Keep at it and be creative. You can and will find a strategy to avoid temptation. Be creative about the strategies and make sure you carry out your plans. You will find that a little creativity and effort will often solve a temptation.

By the time you get to this part of the book, you may have been smoke-free for five days, seven days, ten days, or even longer. Well done! You're doing a great job. And you're probably feeling more and more confident about being a nonsmoker.

But there probably have been several times when you've been tempted to have "just one" cigarette. When the temptation is really high, you may think to yourself, "If I have just one cigarette, it's no big deal."

Don't kid yourself! Even one cigarette is a big deal, and it will hurt your chances of quitting. One cigarette can easily lead to two, and before long, you're buying a pack, and soon a carton.

Having even one cigarette reduces your chances of success. You need to be determined that you will not smoke, not at all – not even a puff.

Most successful quitters, however, have failed a few times before they got it right. For many, relapsing and trying again is part of learning to be a nonsmoker.

So be as determined as you can be. Don't start letting yourself have a cigarette here, a cigarette there. But, if you do have a setback, don't get down on yourself. You are still on your way toward eventually being a nonsmoker.
What Happens if You Slip?

It is not the end of the world. Many people slip up and have a cigarette once or twice, but quickly get back on track. So if you do slip, it doesn't mean that you've failed. If you get down on yourself, you aren't giving yourself a chance. So give yourself a break – learn to forgive yourself.

If you really look at it, quitting is a process and backsliding is just part of this whole process. Just make sure you find out what went wrong that you picked up a cigarette – and next time you'll do better.

Millions of people who have quit smoking slip and smoke. And many of these smokers still end up quitting. Here are some steps that you can take to fight slip-ups:

• Stop smoking immediately.
• Take action. Throw away the cigarettes or leave the place where you smoked. Treat your situation like an emergency and get out of it.

Once you've removed yourself form the situation, look back and consider what went wrong. Where were you? What were you doing? Who were you with? Was it your mood that made you vulnerable?

• Analyze the situation and learn what caused the slip-up.
• Prepare yourself for the next time. Ask yourself what you'll do if this situation happens again.
• If the problem was a temptation that got the best of you, then come up with a specific plan to fight the temptation next time.

If you have been using nicotine replacement therapy, take time now to review the package instructions. Maybe you need an increase in your dosage or follow the suggestions on how to use these products more effectively. If you're unsure, you might contact your doctor or pharmacist for guidance.

It's not always easy to get out of a slip-up. Even one slip can plunge people into a sense of helplessness and a feeling that failure is inevitable.

The reason this happens is that there's a part of you (your "inner culprit") that would actually be relieved by proof that your case is hopeless, and the lapse proves it. Then you can just sit back, relax, recognize the age-old fact that "we all got to go sometime," and simply accept your smoking, and get on with enjoying life.

People know that this isn't really true. We all do "got to go sometime," but smoking makes us go a lot faster than we would have if we didn't smoke.

That is an undeniable medical fact. Perhaps at this stage, you should go back and review all those depressing facts about what smoking does to you, and how it kills you faster.

Don't let your "inner culprit" allow you to justify smoking. Here are two ways of fighting back:

• Recognize that quitting smoking is much more important than most of the other things you do for your health.
• Remember that most ex-smokers relapsed several times before they succeeded, so you're just kidding yourself if you think your case is impossible.

Reviewing Your Progress

It's not easy to break a long-term habit like smoking. But you're doing it! If you've reached this point, you're motivated and determined. But the battle is not won yet. You will have to stay alert.

One way to do this is to monitor your progress each and every day. Get a sheet of paper and at the end of the day, write down all the difficult situations that you faced and the coping strategies that you used successfully. Then make a list of things you will do during the next day, instead of smoking.

113

Get in the habit of reviewing your progress each and every day. This will be a great record of your wonderful achievement, and it will provide you with loads of encouragement that what you're doing actually works, and that you have the ability to fight back and win over the urge to smoke.

Also, don't forget to enjoy the rewards that you promised yourself each week and each month you go without smoking.

Stay alert most of all, because relapses can occur for several months after quitting. Those old associations between cigarettes and all the times you used to smoke have not all gone away. Just as with all the other hard and important things you've done in your life, you need to give this one the attention it deserves until you've really got it licked.

But it is not just struggling and more struggling. Each day you go without smoking puts you another day closer to becoming a confirmed nonsmoker – for life. That will take about 6 months. But think of something that happened 6 months ago. Seems like yesterday, right?

It will get easier and you will get through the next weeks and months to arrive at your goal – nonsmoking – and not missing cigarettes.

## THE FIRST SIX MONTHS

You have done it! You've quit smoking and stayed that way for two whole weeks! That's really great. You probably weren't sure that you could do it, but you were able to. It is a great boost to your health!

Now, the best way to enjoy life without cigarettes is by not smoking for 6 months straight. Although, you have already come a long way, you still need a little help, and this is what this chapter will give. In fact, the first things you've got to do is not to relax too much because you feel so successful.

At this point you may feel that quitting has been easier than you expected. Not that it's been easy altogether, but it still has not been as hard as you feared.

You may now go for several hours, maybe most of the day or evening, without even thinking about a cigarette. But don't get over-confident. Stay alert – because you may find yourself suddenly tempted to smoke, and if your guard is down, you could end up puffing away without even realizing what hit you.

The important thing for the next few months is "vigilance." This doesn't mean that you become obsessed with managing your quitting, but you do have to stay on your toes, so that you're always alert to the temptations or situations that can mess up your plan.

If you do slip-up, just keep going. Don't get depressed and get discouraged. Remember, the average successful quitter relapsed several times before getting it right. Relapsing does not mean you are a failure. Relapsing and relearning from your mistakes and trying again are all part of successful quitting.

More About Temptations

In order to stay a nonsmoker, you will have to keep vigilant and guard against the temptations that could cause you to slip up. Unfortunately temptations will not just disappear. Not for a while. In the first few months, when you see or taste a cup of coffee or make a telephone call, you may just as likely get an urge to have a cigarette, as you did when you were a smoker.

By the time you've been off cigarettes for over two weeks, the frequency of your urges is going way down. But some urges can still be real killers. Here's one consolation: The worst is over! The nicotine is gone from your system, most physical withdrawal symptoms are sharply reduced, and the frequency of those urges and cravings is going down.

That means that the cravings you're experiencing are coming from your mind, not from your body. Try not to be discouraged or frustrated by this. Habits you've had for years are not something that will disappear. The important thing is to recognize where the urges are coming from and to use that knowledge to fight the cravings.

As the months go by, you will notice that even your mental cravings are becoming more like thoughts than strong drives.

Ex-smokers who have been off cigarettes for a long time say that they still have thoughts about cigarettes, but not pressing urges.

So how should you deal with these temptations now that the smoking is out of the question? Practice your creative alternatives and work on your will power.

Now is a good time to reevaluate your temptations and your plans for coping with them. As your physical cravings have decreased, you've probably noticed that the temptations that used to affect you may no longer be the ones that bother you now.

Cigarettes and cigarette packages are still likely to be your strongest temptations. You got rid of all your cigarettes when you quit smoking. But now is the time to do a double check of all the places where you used to keep them. The obvious places and the not-so obvious places. It's important to make sure that you really get rid of every last one, because one of the easiest ways to fall off the wagon (especially when you feel confident that you have mastered your desire for cigarettes) is to come across a couple of leftover cigarettes.

Below is a list of common temptations and what you can do to fight back:

Temptations:

• Having an alcoholic drink
• Watching TV
• Getting ready for a meeting
• Talking on the telephone
• Drinking coffee
• Finishing a meal
• Taking a work break
• The end of the workday

Fighting Back:

• Stretch and touch your toes
• Do deep breathing exercises
• Do a crossword puzzle
• Knit, sew
• Build a model plane, boat, train

- Go for a walk
- Exercise
- Take a shower
- Suck on a stirring stick
- Chew sugarless gum
- Doodle

Also, learn to avoid smoking places and people. This includes smoking sections, bars, restaurants, canteens, bowling alleys and golf courses. It's not only places that present a problem; it's people who smoke. Most relapses begin with a cigarette offered by another smoker.

You are vulnerable to the temptation to join in when someone else lights up. This is especially true when ex-smokers are feeling confident they have their smoking under control. A friend offers them a cigarette, and they figure they can have just one. That's why it will really help during the next few weeks if you avoid people who smoke, even if they're your best friends. Also, try to pass on social situations that involve people who are smokers. It's bad enough when you watch one-person light up, but watching five, ten, or more people can be too strong a temptation.

It might help if you made a list of your friends and acquaintances that smoke. Put your closest smoking friends at the top of the list and your casual smoking friends and acquaintances at the bottom of the list. Then draw a line at that place on the list where your close smoking friends end and your casual smoking friends and acquaintances begin.

The object is not to destroy your friendships. Rather your goal is to spend less time with your smoking friends and a lot less time with casual friends and acquaintances that smoke.

A little will power can help. Anticipating that you will miss being with your friends who smoke, you might plan to talk to them on the phone, or meet them in a nonsmoking setting, like a movie or a stroll through a park.

A lot of relapses occur in social situations. Drinking, talking with friends, feeling relaxed and maybe a little too confident about your smoking, or perhaps feeling a little shy and anxious, and being offered a cigarette – these can cause the strongest person to slip up.

Of course, you cannot avoid all social situations where people may be smoking. But you can get through them without smoking. Here are strategies to keep those temptations from taking over.

1) Shortly before you get to the party, review in your mind your firm decision that you will not smoke, no matter what.

2) Take some time shortly before the party to visualize yourself not smoking in key situations that are likely to occur. Think of what the place will look like. If it includes a meal, try to imagine what will be served. Practice saying, "No, thanks, I quit." This will help to internalize your resolve.

3) To make sure you don't feel anxious or like a wallflower, plan some things you'll talk about, perhaps a funny story you heard or an article you read in the newspaper.

4) Drink something nonalcoholic during the party or limit yourself to one drink.

5) Talk ahead of time to friends who will be there. Tell them you are concerned although determined, and ask them to give you encouragement during the party.

6) Ahead of time, use positive self-talk to affirm your decision not to smoke.

But what if, despite all your precautions and all your assertiveness, you still have trouble with your urges to smoke? What if they get stronger and stronger and you don't think you can hang on much longer? Just leave! Go home. Or go for a walk until your smoking urges have calmed down. Here are some strategies:

• Waiting it out. When your craving is a mild one, it's often possible to wait it out. After 5 or 6 minutes, the urge often fades and disappears.
• Reviewing your most important reasons for quitting smoking. Sine you have been a nonsmoker for a while, you probably will have new reasons for being a nonsmoker. Make sure you write all these down.
• Talking yourself out of an urge. Say to yourself, "This will not last. This will go away. I'm doing really well. This urge won't throw me if I don't let it."
• Thinking away the urge. Recall some of the diseases related to smoking that meant the most to you. Then think how you have lowered your odds of getting them. Then say to yourself, "I will not smoke."
• Do stress release exercises and deep breathing exercises.

Meditation

Now that you no longer have cigarettes to take the edge off of stress, you may want to try meditation. Although meditation is associated with several spiritual traditions, this version is a simple, non-religious one. Here, meditation is simply training you to focus your attention in a way that releases tension. It feels somewhat like dozing, because it causes a drop in your breathing rate and your blood pressure.

Here's how you do it:

1) Sit quietly in a comfortable position in a chair. Or you can sit cross-legged on a bed or on the floor if you like, but it's not necessary.

2) Close your eyes.

3) Consciously try to relax all your muscles as much as you can.

4) Breathe through your nose, and each time you breathe out, say the word "one" (or choose another simple word).

Focus your mind on the word "one" as you're saying it. If ideas come into your head that distract you, just notice them a little, and then bring your mind slowly and easily back to the word "One." Don't try too hard to focus your attention in any one direction. You want to go with what comes to mind, while you gently work your way back to "one."

Do these meditations exercise once or twice a day for 15 to 20 minutes in a place where you can be alone. Using meditation and the other breathing techniques will help you cope not only with tension related to quitting smoking, but with tension in general. In fact, you may find these techniques helpful even when your smoking days are long gone.

Discontinuing Nicotine Replacement

As your sense of control increases, you may want to think about discontinuing the use of any nicotine replacement products you've been using. As times goes on since your last cigarette, you will no longer need to rely on nicotine gum, patches, sprays or inhalers.

When you start thinking about getting off sprays or medication it may be a good time to check in with your doctor, who will be happy to hear about your progress and might be able to help you in planning to discontinue the nicotine replacement products.

If you have been using nicotine gum or patches (which are sold without a prescription) you can begin the weaning process yourself. You can take the following approach:

Nicotine Gum: Use nicotine gum every day for at least two to three months after quitting. If you have successfully stayed off smoking for that time, you will be able to gradually reduce the number of pieces of the gum you use each day.

When you get down to just one or two pieces a day, you can stop using it. But continue to carry some with you for a few more weeks, in case of an emergency situation that might tempt you to smoke. Here is a good plan to follow:

• Reduce one piece a day for five days. If you feel any withdrawal symptoms during the week, don't decrease the next day. Instead, stay at one level for one week. Then begin to decrease again. After five days of decreasing, stay at the level for one week.
• Repeat the above procedure until you get to one or two pieces a day. Stay at one or two a day for one week, and then quit.
• As you cut down, cut the pieces in half or replace one or more pieces with regular, sugar-free gum.
• Start chewing the pieces for only half the time. This will help you break the chewing habit, if you need to.

Design your plan so that you will be completely free and confident of your freedom from nicotine in six months. For most smokers, that means starting to cut down on nicotine gum after three months of use.

Nicotine Patches: Many people prefer the simplicity of a single strength patch. But some patches come in different sizes and shapes. The larger the patch, the more nicotine it delivers through the skin. Many smokers start with the strongest patch. Then after several weeks, they can switch to a medium strength patch for a few weeks, and possibly a lower strength patch for the last few weeks.

Patches are available for either six-week or ten-week treatment periods. They are usually not meant to be used for more than three months.

Although some people are able to stop using nicotine patches at this point without tapering-off period, a gradual dose reduction is often recommended.

If you are using a brand of patches that come in several dosage levels, taper off by switching to the next lower dose for two weeks. If an even lower dose is available, switch to that for your last two weeks. If you are using a single-strength patch, you can try wearing the patch for only half a day, or skipping every other day, then skipping two days, and so on.

Whichever tapering approach you decide on, be sure to err on the side of using the patch for a longer rather than a shorter period of time. Generally, the entire course of the nicotine patch use and gradual tapering-off should take no more than 14 to 20 weeks.

You might wonder if it is hard to give up the nicotine patch after so much time. Studies have shown that it is much easier to give up the patch than it is to give up cigarettes, for two reasons:

• One of the reasons smoking is so attractive is that the nicotine reaches the brain in about 7 seconds. With the patch, the nicotine level in your body stays relatively constant day after day. There is no immediate "hit," so little craving develops.

• In smoking, all the things that you are doing while you smoke become linked to the nicotine "hit." Talking on the phone, drinking coffee – these all develop strong links to nicotine. Since you put on the patch only one a day, and receive a steady stream of nicotine, no links are developed.

Nicotine Nasal Spray and Nicotine Inhalers. You may have been getting nicotine administered via a nasal spray or by the newest method, an inhaler. Both of these are prescription products. Your doctor will give you instructions on weaning yourself from these. Recommended strategies include:

• Use half a dose at a time.
• Use the spray or inhaler less frequently.
• Skip every other dose for several days. Continue to skip doses on succeeding days.

Prescription Medication: If you have been taking the "non-nicotine pill" Zyban, which is available only by prescription, your doctor may have provided only a seven or eight week supply. Some studies have found that extending treatment beyond eight weeks does not increase the pill's effectiveness.

So, your health care professional may want to wean you off the non-nicotine pill at this point, if you have successfully stopped smoking.

However, longer treatment may be advised if your cravings are not yet controlled well enough to guard against a possible relapse.

Am I Done Yet?

By this time, you're probably wondering, "When will all this stop smoking routine end?" Well, the answer is, "Not just yet!"

There's still more to do, but you do deserve tremendous praise for your successful progress so far. Now is the time to look at how far you have come:

• You gained an understanding of your habit and your addiction to nicotine, and you learned to identify your smoking temptations.
• You gained the resolve to decide to quit.
• You developed your personalized quitting plan.
• You learned how to break your habits, deal with temptations, and get the cooperation you needed in preparation for your Quit Day.
• You took the big step – your Quit Day – and you successfully managed the first 24 hours.
• You worked on managing symptoms of physical and psychological recovery from nicotine during your first two weeks as a nonsmoker, and you learned how to treat slip-ups as an emergency.
• And finally you learned long-term strategies for staying vigilant against smoking temptations.

When you get to six months after your Quit Day, you obviously have a lot to be proud of. And you probably won't have any problems recognizing your own accomplishments, and feeling great in another six months when you make one year.

So enjoy it. You really deserve it. You've done a wonderful job. You've accomplished something that was very hard, but very, very worthwhile.

Now is the time for making one more list. On a piece of paper, or on your computer, put down what you think are the most important things you want to keep in your mind to make sure you don't get into trouble with smoking in the future.

Maybe it's all your reasons for quitting smoking in the first place. Also, keep in mind the method's you used to maintain your vigilance.

Maybe it's one particular creative alternative that you used, or a will power strategy. Maybe you've begun walking every day, and have come to love it, and want to make sure you never give it up.

Maybe you've learned new ways to cope with anxiety or sadness, or maybe you've learned some skills for being less shy or more assertive.

Whatever it is, write it down, so you can have a list of your wonderful accomplishments.

# DEALING WITH WEIGHT GAIN

As you're going through the quitting process, you may have got on your bathroom scales and noticed that you've gained some weight. Many ex-smokers do gain weight after quitting. In fact, concern about weight gain is a real hurdle for most people. It's the reason many smokers are afraid to quit. And when smokers do quit, if they gain weight, they often go back to smoking to losing weight.

Of course, this is an unrealistic concern for most smokers. The degree of weight gain is relatively small in most cases.

To reach the same health risk as smoking one pack of cigarette per day, the average smoker would have to be roughly 125 pounds overweight!

Why Ex-Smokers Gain Weight

Smokers weigh less because smoking depresses the appetite for certain foods, while quitters, whose appetites are not suppressed, gain weight because they take in more calories.

While food intake may not be the only factor operating – nicotine may also alter the smoker's metabolism so that smokers burn more calories and convert fewer calories into fat.

Smoking also affects digestion. Research has shown that food remains in the stomachs of smokers longer than it does in nonsmokers. Fullness of the stomach signals to the brain that you don't need to eat.

This could be one of the ways that smoking tends to reduce smokers' body weight. Some other reasons for smokers not gaining weight are:

• Smoking provides the smoker with a substitute activity for eating.
• Smoking increases the passage of food through the lower digestive tract by increasing the propulsive activity of the colon. Thus, some food may be swept through before all nutrients are absorbed.
• Smoking serves as a marker of the end of a meal. Rather than taking a second or third helping or having dessert, smokers are likely to stop eating and have a cigarette.

Recent studies of certain enzymes in our fat cells suggest that the reason some smokers gain weight after quitting while others do not may be in part a matter of genetics. One of the key enzymes in the regulation of fat storage is lipoprotein lipase. This enzyme breaks down circulating triglycerides, liberating free fatty acids that can then be taken up and stored by the fat cells.

High activity levels of this enzyme are thought to increase the efficiency of fat storage, and thus to produce weight gain. Low levels are thought to produce less efficient energy storage, and thus to promote weight loss.

Researchers believe that genetic differences account for high or low levels of lipoprotein lipase in different people.

Studies have also shown that smokers with high levels of lipoprotein lipase gained more weight after they quit, while smokers with the lowest levels of this enzyme actually lost weight after quitting.

The researchers concluded that a test that measured lipoprotein lipase activity might help predict a smoker's potential for weight gain after quitting.

Another factor contributing to lower body weight in smokers could be impaired lung function.

Research suggests that it is only those smokers with the most extensive smoking-produced lung damage who exhibited weight loss. The researchers found that smokers with normal lung function weighed roughly the same as nonsmokers.

Another recent study found that smokers who consumed more food or liquids, or avoided other cigarette-associated substances such as alcohol and coffee, were more successful in cutting down their smoking than subjects who attempted to reduce smoking with no specific plan. Thus weight gain following quitting may be due to the fact that the quitters are using eating as a substitute for smoking.

Here are some points that will help you control your weight as you quit smoking.

1) Ignore weight gain. Go ahead and quit. After all, you may be one of the lucky ones who gain little or no weight. This is a good approach for light smokers and those who would not be greatly upset by gaining a few pounds. If you take this approach, go ahead and get yourself permanently separated from cigarettes. So don't worry about it, and go ahead and quit.

2) Use exercise to control weight. Quitting really takes all your energy and effort, so the best way to use exercise to help control weight after quitting might be to begin a regular exercise program, several months before your planned quitting date. Exercise will help you keep your weight down, and it can also make it easier for you to quit and will provide you with an alternative activity that will help you make it through the most difficult parts of cigarette withdrawal.

3) The sugar-free solution. As with exercise, it's difficult to quit smoking and to change your eating patterns at the same time.

The best guideline here seems to be to start taking control of your eating before you quit. Here are some good foods to stock up on:

• Fruit juices
• Sunflower seeds
• Spring or mineral water
• Carrots
• Popcorn (without butter)
• Yogurt (low-fat, unsweetened)
• V-8 juice
• Apples
• Bananas
• Dry-roasted peanuts

4) Pay special attention to your mealtime routine during your pre-quitting and quitting efforts. Here are some mealtime tips to help ex-smokers watch their weight:

• Take smaller portions (use a smaller plate).
• Eat slowly. Try to be the last one done.
• Take smaller bites. Chew and swallow each bite before taking the next. Become aware of the taste and texture of your food.
• Put your fork down between mouthfuls.
• Pour yourself a large glass of ice water with every meal. Take frequent sips between bites.
• Have a family member prepare your portions and put extra food away so that seconds are not easily accessible.
• Serve sliced fruit for dessert – or skip dessert altogether.
• As soon as you finish, get up from the table.
• Pick a nonsmoking activity to be a sign of meal termination. Take a walk, brush your teeth, wash the dishes, take a shower, puff on a plastic cigarette, eat an artificially sweetened mint, or develop your own meal termination ritual.

## Between-Meal Solutions

Recent quitters frequently experience strong urges to snack or have something in their mouths. If sweets are available you may feel a powerful urge to nibble.

You may also feel an urge to hold something in place of a cigarette. Here are some tips to help you avoid overdoing it on high-sugar snacks:

• Allow yourself unlimited amounts of raw vegetables, such as carrot or celery sticks, cherry tomatoes, cucumber slices, broccoli flowerets, cauliflower buds, etc. Keep these in the front of the refrigerator where they are easily accessible.
• Always carry a good supply of sugarless gum, mints, and candy. Eat only one piece of candy or gum at a time and try to make each piece last as long as possible.
• Allow yourself moderate amounts of low-calorie snacks, such as bread sticks, unbuttered popcorn, pretzels, etc. Avoid snacks that contain large amounts of sugar or fat.
• Stay away from alcohol. Alcoholic beverages are high in calories. Also, alcohol can produce breakdowns in self-control that may lead to eating binges or a smoking relapse.
• Unshelled sunflower seeds or unshelled peanuts are particularly good snacks. They keep both your hands and your mouth busy, and the process of removing the shell slows down how much you eat.
• Don't keep high calorie snacks in the house for 3-6 months after you quit. If this is not possible, seal high-calorie snacks in plastic bags and put them in a hard-to-reach cupboard.
• Ask friends and family not to offer you food.
• When you feel the urge to snack, go for a walk instead.
• During the early stages of quitting, avoid parties where high-calorie snacks will be served.
• Take healthy snacks with you when you will be away from home.

• Go to bed earlier than usual to avoid the temptation to snack.
• Keep yourself busy with hobbies, puzzles, knitting, gardening, creative crafts, housework, home repairs, etc.

In order to keep your weight down, here are useful tips that you should use to help you along:

• If possible, don't set your Quit Day shortly before holidays when it is usual to eat high-calories foods and drinks. The temptation to munch may be too hard to resist.
• Weight Watchers or other such groups can be a big help in your efforts to control your weight. The best time to join such a group is before you quit.
• Weigh yourself daily, at the same time every day. Record your daily weight on a chart or calendar. This will make you more aware of weight changes.
• Drink plenty of liquids such as mineral water, iced tea, iced coffee, or diet sodas.

Realistic Goals for Weight Control

The problem of smoking and its effect on weight control can be especially difficult for people who feel that they have a weight problem even with smoking. In this case, you have to be realistic and say to yourself what is more important your health or a few extra pounds, which you can work towards losing at a later date. For smokers who want to quit and don't want to make changes in their eating habits, the best course of action is to go ahead and let yourself gain those extra pounds. Being a few pounds overweight is a lot healthier than smoking.

You may quit, gain five pounds, go back to smoking, lose the five pounds, quit smoking and regain those five pounds. Here's how you can get off this vicious cycle:

• First of all, quit smoking for good.
• Work to recognize that the weight gain is less important than staying off the cigarettes. Consider buying some health books or magazines that will help give you healthy choices to follow.
• Don't worry about eating less. Concentrate on eating more healthily and exercising more.
• When you can cut back on calories without finding yourself tempted to smoke, you can start planning how to lose the weight.

In short, you need to solve the smoking problem first, and then work on the weight when you can do so without triggering those strong urges to smoke.

If you're still gaining weight after being successfully off cigarettes for a month or more, then you could be reaching for food whenever you get the urge to smoke. Instead of eating, try drinking non-alcoholic liquids. Keep a glass of water, club soda, juice, or diet soda handy throughout the day.

Overall, you should eat more healthy foods. Think about what you eat; this way you will overcome your desire for fatty foods and sweets.

Here's what to do:

• Eat more lean meat and fish. Lean meats such as veal, chicken, and turkey are low in fat and calories and high in vitamins and minerals. The same is true of fish.
• Eat more fruits and vegetables. The FDA advises that you "Strive for Five" which means that you should have at least five servings of fruits and vegetables each day.
• Eat less sugar. If you take in more sugar than the body needs, the excess sugar is converted into body fat. Sugar is an obvious ingredient in cookies, cakes, candy, and also hides in many canned and frozen convenience foods.

Check the labels on the products you buy for: Glucose, sucrose, and other sugars.
• Cut down on fat. Use low-fat milk, yogurt, and cottage cheese instead of whole-milk products. Trim fat from meats. Broil, bake or steam instead of frying foods in fat.
• Go easy on alcohol. Alcohol doesn't provide nutrients, but it does provide a high dose of calories.
• Eat three square meals a day. Skipping breakfast and lunch will not help you control your weight, but is liable to give you headaches, jitters, and a ravenous appetite that may lead you to binge or look for a cigarette. Eating three moderate meals through the day will make you feel better, will get your metabolism going better, and will probably result in your having fewer total calories than if you skip a meal or two.
• Eat the right snacks. Good choices are foods that take a long time to chew, like apples, unbuttered popcorn, carrots, and celery sticks.
• Cook with herbs and spices. That way you'll use less butter, margarine, oil or fattening sauces.
• Start your meals right. Have a clear soup, or an "undressed" salad, or a low-calorie drink (water, seltzer, tomato juice, tea) before eating a meal. It will help fill you up.

What you do and don't do is just as important as what you eat or don't eat. For example, do get lots of exercise. That will burn calories, cut stress, and make you feel good. Also, do eat when you're hungry, not when you're bored. And finally, when you're through eating, get up. Don't sit there thinking about dessert – or a cigarette.

You may be looking at the scale every day and worrying about your weight. But have you been looking in the mirror? If not, take a look right now! Have you noticed any changes? Many ex-smokers notice that their color is better, their teeth are whiter, and their eyes are brighter.

# BECOMING A NONSMOKER FOREVER

Over 1000 Americans die every day of smoking-related diseases. Quitting reduces or eliminates all of the harmful effects of smoking. But all, too many who quit, go back to smoking.

Quitting smoking takes practice. It takes more practice for some people than for others. In fact, almost everyone who tries to quit slips up once or twice and smokes a cigarette.

Having a couple of cigarettes is one thing. It's a slip-up. And you should not get depressed over the fact that you had a cigarette. But having a couple, then a couple more, then a couple each day –is quite another thing.

Before you know it, you're back to smoking at least a few cigarettes every day. It's a judgment call, but at that point you've probably gone from slip to relapse.

If you realize that you have relapsed, don't get down on yourself. It doesn't mean you've failed. Give yourself a break. And forgive yourself. Millions of people who have quit smoking don't succeed on the first try, or even a second or third try. Mark Twain said: "Quitting smoking is easy. I've done it hundreds of times."

But many ex-smokers who relapse do end up quitting for good. So each time you try to quit, you make a real step forward. Research has shown that those who try to quit make at least five unsuccessful attempts. Most of these smokers who tried to quit started smoking again within a month's time.

Many said they began smoking again because they faced a stressful situation and needed a cigarette to cope. Being around others who smoke was also a common reason for resuming the smoking habit.

## How to Get Back on Track

If your most recent attempt didn't succeed, what can you do about your smoking now? You have two choices:

• If you have smoked just a few cigarettes for two or three days, and you feel you had made some good progress toward successfully quitting, treat this setback as a temporary slip. Stop smoking immediately! Throw away all your cigarettes! Find out what went wrong, and do better this time around. Remember, this is an emergency. You must act now.
• If you have gone back to smoking several cigarettes a day for more than a couple of days, you may conclude that you have relapsed. At this point, you need to decide whether to re-start your quitting program immediately, or take a few days' break to get your thoughts together.

What is important is the fact that you must quit with determination and clarity. You may do better if you take some time to gather your thoughts, review your reasons and plans for quitting and start over.

Keep in mind the following facts:

• Slips and relapses are often part of the path to success.
• Half of the smokers (millions of heavy smokers) have already quit.
• Quitting is more important than the other things you do for your health.
• You really want to quit!

If you have relapses, you should consider sticking to your commitment to quit. You should do an immediate re-start, to get right back on track. You have invested considerable time and effort in your success thus far.

You may not have finished your plan, but you have made a good start! Don't give up now!

After all, your time off cigarettes has already cleared much of the nicotine out of your system. You've survived the worst days of nicotine withdrawal. And you've already had some good practice in coping with smoking triggers and in using creative alternatives to give your substitutes for cigarettes when you get the urge to light up.

Fast Way to Re-Quit!

Every cigarette you don't smoke, every time you say, "No!" is a small victory. Every small victory helps you beat your old smoking habit. Practice makes perfect. If you slipped up, it means you didn't quite handle a temptation you faced. It doesn't mean that you are a failure or that you are addicted and can't quit.

So before you go any further, add up your victories:

• On a calendar, check off the days you went without cigarettes.
• Record the days on which you smoked one, two, or more cigarettes.
• Give the reason why you smoked.
• Write down what steps you could have taken that might have helped you to avoid smoking in that situation.

The goal is to pinpoint what went wrong each time you slipped and had a cigarette. Forget guilt and blame. Instead, focus on what caused the slips and what you will do differently next time.

For example, you may find that your slips occurred only in the evening when you were home relaxing and watching television.

An alternative can be that you have some substitutes ready while watching television in the evening, perhaps busy work or some hobby you can do at the same time, or perhaps some reasonably healthy snacks.

Long-term, successful ex-smokers almost never puff. Virtually all of them feel that it's easier to have none, than one.

Mental Preparation

When you first decided to quit smoking, you began the process of learning to be a nonsmoker. You thought about the benefits smoking had offered you (such as stress relief, weight control, and social acceptance). You also became aware of the negatives (the health risks, the expense, the loss of control over your life).

Then you identified alternative activities you could use to replace smoking in your life. The next step was to begin practicing those alternatives.

You've had some practice over the past few weeks, but you're still learning. This learning stage will continue until you get really good at nonsmoking. That usually takes at least several weeks, but often two or three months.

So if you've stumbled recently, it doesn't mean you can't accomplish your goal. It simply means you will have to continue in the intensive learning stage for at least another month or two.

You will probably go back to smoking if you tell yourself too often that you're deprived. So talk to yourself. Talk about the benefits of not smoking.

Remind yourself that you are healthier now that you are a nonsmoker.

Remember, this has been a great accomplishment. You will begin to like yourself as a nonsmoker. It's in your power to let either deprivation or determination take over. The best thing to tell yourself is: "I can do it! I can keep myself from smoking!"

When you're in a difficult situation and feel like smoking, tell yourself, "The urge will pass whether I smoke or not." If you're at a social gathering and someone tempts you by offering you a cigarette, think to yourself, "I can say, No! I feel good when I stand up for what I believe in."

Here are some things to say to yourself when you want to smoke:

• "The urge will pass whether I smoke or not."
• "I'm not going through the pain of quitting again!"
• "I like my body when I'm not smoking."
• "I'll distract myself until the urge passes."
• "I deserve credit for quitting smoking."

If you've ever participated in sports, you will understand the value of this mental preparation. Just as athletes get mentally ready for a big event, you will have to "psych yourself up" for the smoking challenges you'll face each day.

Visualization is another tool that athletes use. They "see" themselves scoring the winning run or clearing the high hurdle.

In the same way, you can visualize yourself as having achieved the goal you have in mind – becoming a nonsmoker. Then act as if it were true.

Here's how you can do it:

• Choose a positive phrase you are willing to repeat to yourself each day.

• Visualize yourself in a new situation and continue to repeat that phrase until you begin to believe it.

Here are a few examples of phrases that you can use:

• "I feel better since I've stopped smoking."
• I feel a lot more in control of myself."
• I am so glad that my world no longer revolves around cigarettes."
• There's nothing that could ever get me to go back to smoking."
• I'm doing this because I finally decided I want to."

Encouragement From Family and Friends

Just as athletes rely on team members and encourage each other, you also have a team – your family and friends – who will cooperate and encourage you in your efforts to win. Take time to talk with your family and friends.

At this point, you probably have a better idea of who is really helpful in guiding you around temptations, or just understanding what you're going through. Follow these leads. Make a point of getting more of their encouragement.

If you have one key family member or friend whom you've looked to for help, review how that's gone. Because you've slipped up in your nonsmoking plan, you may have hesitated to keep in touch with that person.

Maybe you're too embarrassed to call and admit your problems. But chances are good that your key person will be a lot more understanding than you may fear.

If your friends or family are ex-smokers, they will know how good it feels and will be happy to give you all the encouragement they can. And if they had trouble quitting, they can make you feel understood. Maybe with their help you can come up with new strategies to help you win.

Also, think about your family situation. Under the best of circumstances, your family members will be rooting for you all the way. But maybe your spouse or your parents are smokers themselves, and they may unknowingly resent your efforts, or feel guilty about not trying to quit with you.

If this has been a problem in your family, it could be the reason you've had trouble staying off cigarettes. Studies show, for example, that those who fail to quit or who relapse are more likely to be married to a smoking spouse and/or to have many friends and family members who smoke.

Try to think of your quitting as separate from your family's smoking. It's their right to smoke, and it's your right to quit. You cannot make your spouse or family members quit smoking. So focus on cooperation and support from other family and friends who don't smoke.

But of course you don't want to avoid the people you love. Try to separate your quitting from their smoking. Make them cooperate and not angry.

You can still expect your family to cooperate with your quitting. You might want to negotiate with them about:

• Limiting their smoking in specific situations that are heavy temptations for you, like in the kitchen after dinner. You can't ask them not to smoke, but you can identify situations in which it would be a big help if they didn't smoke.
• When it's possible, ask them to smoke outside the house (perhaps on the front porch, back patio, or terrace). But it's their house too, so you may want to take a walk when they're smoking. Try to keep this friendly and cooperative, not demanding.
• When they do smoke inside, ask them to smoke in rooms that have windows or fans to send the smoke outside.

• Ask them not to smoke in the car.
• Ask them to sit with you in nonsmoking areas.

Some of this may seem like asking a lot. But when you think about it, quitting smoking is such an advantage for your health that it doesn't make too much sense for others to do anything that will stand in your way. But attitudes and family patterns change slowly.

Also, your smoking relatives may be so conscious of their own wishes to stop smoking (whether or not they acknowledge it) that asking them to limit their smoking, or even the fact that you're quitting, may annoy them. So you will need to cooperate and compromise with your family.

One approach that may be helpful is to stress that you are just asking them to cooperate with you for the first month or so, while you get used to life without cigarettes. It's not that you are asking them never to smoke in front of you again.

What Else You Can Do

Smokers who are thinking of quitting often worry that they will be too stressed out, or that they will gain too much weight. Did this happen to you? If so, go back to the sections on stress management and weight control in this book.

Exercise is a good remedy for both problems. So if you haven't been getting regular exercise, think about doing about 30 minutes (three times a week) of moderate exercise.

Even going for a daily walk for fifteen or thirty minutes is great exercise. It's a stress fighter and a creative alternative during the times when you otherwise might light up.

You don't need elaborate equipment to exercise. You don't even need to join a gym (although it is a good idea, if it appeals to you). Just get out and walk, or ride a bike, or go for a swim. The idea is to have fun – active fun.

One other tool that you can use to help yourself is to plan rewards and celebrations. Right now, you may tend to be a bit hard on yourself. Maybe you thought about rewards for your progress, but if you've had some slips, you may really think there's not much to celebrate now.

This is just the time to consider a different approach. Maybe you need to lighten up and go easy on yourself. You probably have made a lot more progress than you would have thought a month or two ago. See if you can get into a generous spirit with yourself and give yourself the credit you deserve for the progress you've made.

Forget about words like failure or will power. You haven't failed; you're still practicing. Use rewards to help you set small goals. Don't let small victories go by unnoticed. It reminds you that you've done far too much work to go back to smoking.

Starting Over

If you feel you need a break before tackling quitting again, that's not a problem. Remember, the average person who succeeds as a nonsmoker may quit a few times and then relapse before finally getting it right. You can learn from your relapse, regroup, and get it right.

Although you feel that you're not ready to quit right now, don't put the thought out of your mind. Before you forget, take a few notes about your experience this time, so you'll have something to build on next time. Here are some questions to ask yourself:

• What was the best part of my effort?
• What did I do that was most helpful?
• As I was working on quitting what reasons for quitting and benefits seemed most important or meaningful to me?
• What problems turned up that I didn't expect?
• Was I bothered by a major life change or stress that is unlikely to occur in the future?
• Where did I get cigarettes when I slipped up? Did someone give me one? Or did I find a hidden stash at home or at the office?
• What do I think is the most important thing for me to remember the next time I quit?

Here are some other factors to consider in trying to learn from your efforts:

1) Timing. Maybe the time of the year wasn't right for you to quit. If you quit in the summer this time around, when you take vacations and have lots of free time, you might want to plan your next Quit Date for the winter, when your time and activities are more structured.

2) Quitting group. Some people enjoy and do well working together with others who are also trying to quit. Next time, you might try joining a group program. Look for your local chapter of the American Lung Association for clinics in your area.

3) Nicotine replacement. If you did not use nicotine replacement products this time (nicotine gum, patches, nasal spray or nicotine inhaler), you might want to consider doing so next time.

Some of these products are available over-the-counter, without a prescription. If you did use nicotine replacement and it didn't help enough, ask yourself whether:

• You should have used it longer, or used a stronger dosage.

• You used it correctly.
• You may have relied too heavily on the nicotine replacement and not enough on doing things to organize your quitting, maximize your motivation, and combat temptation.

Nicotine replacement is not a "magic tonic." You may want to consult your doctor or pharmacist on this. You might also ask them if other medications might be helpful for you, like Zyban.

4) Doctor's advice. Just because you don't need a prescription for nicotine gum or nicotine patches, doesn't mean you should not consider seeing your doctor. If you didn't check with your doctor this time, you might plan to do so the next time you're ready to quit. Your doctor may also advise you to use one of the prescription nicotine replacement products, such as nicotine spray or inhaler.

5) Weight gain. Did increased weight cause you to go back to smoking? That's a common occurrence. You might want to speak with a nutritionist to plan a weight-control diet. That way, you'll have weight control tools ready the next time you quit.

6) Exercise. It can be a real help. If you haven't exercised much, it may have been hard to get it started at the same time you were trying to quit. You might want to start an exercise plan now, before quitting again. Then, when you quit, you'll have exercise to fall back on.

7) Moods and relapses. Many people relapse when they are feeling anxious or sad. If that's what happened to you, you might want to work on your stress management. Lots of people control their moods by smoking.

When they quit, they can be surprised that they have feelings of real sadness or anxiety that they hadn't realized before. It shows how effective nicotine is in blocking feelings.

Consult your health care provider, or see a counselor if you're having problems with your feelings after you quit.

Finally take the time to think about the pros and cons of quitting smoking. When you try again, you want to be clear on your own reasons for wanting to quit. And you want to be clear that you want to quit, not that someone or something is driving you to it.

A half-hearted, renewed attempt to quit is likely to end in relapse, which runs the risk of lowering your motivation and confidence. Give your quitting the attention it and you deserve.

Start fresh – go back through all the previous chapters so that you will be clear that you want to quit smoking and that you're confident that you will quit smoking.

You have already made a lot of progress and learned a lot.

## LIVING SMOKE FREE

You've made some significant changes in your life. But quitting smoking is tricky business. In one way, it is very simple – you simply stop putting those white cylinders to your lips. But it is also very complicated.

You had used smoking to cope with all sorts of challenges, from feeling energetic in the morning, to getting out of a bad mood during the middle of the day, to calming down before trying to go to sleep. Smoking was woven into many different areas in your life.

Having quit, you have learned to look at yourself and your habits in a whole new way. And because quitting smoking was so hard, you may feel a particular sense of pride or satisfaction in your ability to have really done it.

One of the reasons this is especially true is because quitting smoking requires the vigilance mentioned earlier. You have found that you need to stay off cigarettes every day to stay quit. This has required an extraordinary commitment on your part.

Often meeting one challenge makes us feel more confident in our ability to meet others. This certainly applies to quitting smoking.

What you've accomplished is a lot harder than most of the goals people set for themselves, such as to exercise more, eat healthier foods, or get their taxes done early.

Now that you feel like a success with quitting smoking, you may want to take on some other challenges you've been hesitant about.

If you gained more weight than you wanted to in quitting, now may be the time to begin focusing your attention on losing it. But a word of caution: it is far more important to stay off cigarettes than to lose 10 or even 20 pounds that you may have gained. So if working on losing weight makes you want to smoke, stop worrying about your weight until you have completely destroyed your urges to smoke.

Make sure you tell your doctor that you have quit smoking. Don't get mad just because your doctor does not remember that you were trying to quit. Most doctors do not keep track of their patients who are trying to quit. That's why you should bring up the subject. There are several good reasons for this.

First, the fact that you've quit may help your doctor and you discover how being a nonsmoker can improve other problems for which you are treated. Your doctor might also want to change or adjust some of your medications now that you're no longer smoking.

Second, if you've gained some weight, you want to make sure the doctor knows it's "for a good cause" – especially if you have diabetes, hypertension, or a history of heart disease. It's important for your doctor to know your weight gain has come about from quitting smoking. Otherwise, you may be pressured to lose it too soon, which could jeopardize your new status as a nonsmoker.

Another reason to tell your doctor is to encourage the two of you to take other steps to improve your health. Doctors love working with patients who do things to help themselves. When your doctor finds out you've quit smoking, he or she will be happy to work with you further to improve your health.

If you are trying to tell someone you care about how much you would like them to quit, you might try a simple statement like:

"I like you (or love you, or care about you) and want to have a lot of time with you. But I'm afraid smoking could take you away much too soon."

They will not be insulted by your telling them you'd like to spend more time with them. And the statement of your fear of losing them makes your point without making them feel you are telling them what to do. You might want to end with a simple offer of help:

"I'd be willing to do whatever I can to help if you want to try it."

But make sure that this does not sound like nagging.
If they look away when you proudly announce that you've made it three months without a cigarette, you will need a subtle approach.

Try telling them four things:

You would never try to push them to quit.

You really were unsure about it, but now you are glad you quit.

What got you serious about quitting was realizing that smoking is so much more dangerous than all the other things we do to ourselves.

You'd be happy to talk to them about it, if they ever thought that would be helpful.

So be kind to smokers. Most (about 90%) would like to quit and wish they'd never started. Your goal now is to help them quit, just as this Book has helped you quit.

# Anything Is Possible

# CONCLUSION

Congratulations! You have tackled something incredibly difficult. You are a nonsmoker. Your self-esteem and confidence is sky-high. You deserve to feel happy and proud about what you've accomplished.

You have taken the time to learn a lot of skills – will power, relaxation, and most important of all, recognizing what you really want and working to achieve it. All of these can be helpful in many other areas of your life.

You have also learned personal and interpersonal communication skills that can improve the quality of your life. These skills will help you bring renewed energy to important things you can do with your life, your family, your children, and your world. That is the most important reward of quitting smoking!

You are probably feeling greatly energized by your experience and you might want to direct some of that energy toward preventing today's young people from starting to smoke. If so, the American Lung Association needs your help in their grassroots tobacco-control initiatives.

Volunteers from around the country are working to keep cigarettes out of the hands of children. Call the American Lung Association at 1-800-LUNG-USA, or visit their web site at http://www.lungusa.org for the latest news and details as to how you can help others stay off cigarettes.